BALLI BALLI

QUICK KOREAN RECIPES FOR EVERY DAY

DA-HAE WEST

PHOTOGRAPHY BY CLARE WINFIELD

RYLAND PETERS & SMALL

Senior Designer Megan Smith
Senior Editor Abi Waters
Head of Production Patricia Harrington
Creative Director Leslie Harrington
Editorial Director Julia Charles
Food Stylist Jennifer Joyce
Prop Stylist Max Robinson
Indexer Cathy Heath

First published in 2025 by
Ryland Peters & Small
20–21 Jockey's Fields, London
WC1R 4BW
and
1452 Davis Bugg Road
Warrenton, NC 27589

www.rylandpeters.com
email: euregulations@rylandpeters.com

10 9 8 7 6 5 4 3 2 1

Text © Da-Hae West 2025
Design and photography
© Ryland Peters & Small 2025

ISBN: 978-1-78879-678-1

Printed in China.

A CIP record for this book is available
from the British Library.

US Library of Congress cataloging-in-
Publication Data has been applied for.

The authorised representative in the EEA
is Authorised Rep Compliance Ltd.,
Ground Floor, 71 Lower Baggot Street,
Dublin, D02 P593, Ireland
www.arccompliance.com

NOTES
• All spoon measurements are level
unless otherwise specified.
• All eggs are medium (UK) or large
(US), unless specified as large, in which
case US extra-large should be used.
Uncooked or partially cooked eggs should
not be served to the very old, frail, young
children, pregnant women or those with
compromised immune systems.
• When a recipe calls for cling film/plastic
wrap, you can substitute for beeswax
wraps, silicone stretch lids or compostable
baking paper for greater sustainability.
• When a recipe calls for the grated zest
of citrus fruit, buy unwaxed fruit and
wash well before using.
• Ovens should be preheated to the
specified temperatures.

CONTENTS

BALLI BALLI
QUICKLY QUICKLY

It's been almost 10 years since my husband and I first started a street-food business in London selling Korean fast food – and a lot has changed since then. The 'Korean Wave,' or *Hallyu* as it's known in Korean, has been more than a quick fad with the interest in Korean pop, TV dramas and food exploding over the last decade. We started the business at a time when people were just beginning to discover Korean food and it was still tricky to get hold of ingredients unless you were lucky enough to live close to a Korean supermarket.

These days, it's possible to pop to your local supermarket and pick up a tub of *gochujang* (Korean red pepper paste) or *ramyun* instant noodles. In fact, my local corner shop even sells the famous *Buldak* fire chicken noodles. We now often hear Korean bands on the radio, with Seventeen on the main stage at Glastonbury Festival and Blackpink headlining Coachella in the US. Korean shops are popping up everywhere – from makeup, to bakeries, to Korean corner shops. The growing interest in all things Korean seems to get bigger each year and it's so exciting to see.

Personally, a lot has changed for me, too. We started the Korean street food business at a time before we had kids, and now we have two wonderful boys. We decided shortly after our eldest was born that street food was too tricky to juggle with young children, so we decided to sell the business. Since then, I've been running Korean cookery classes and writing recipes, as well as juggling life with two young boys, but two years ago, I had to put my life on pause.

After a busy week of teaching cookery classes and hosting food demos, I suddenly found myself in A&E with what turned out to be a benign brain tumour. Things were a bit of a whirlwind and after a couple of months in hospital after two surgeries, I was able to come home. When my tumour was diagnosed, my parents were in Korea but they thankfully rushed back. While Gareth kept our kids' lives as normal as possible during this crazy time, my mum kept my fridge stocked with kimchi, *banchan* (side dishes) and a freezer full of nourishing soups. In Korea, food is more than just sustenance – it is culture, medicine and, more than anything, it is love, and although I wouldn't say that my family are overly cuddly, they definitely express their love through food. It was an incredible comfort to be able to reach in the fridge and eat my mum's cooking.

It took me a little over six months to feel even close to normal again. My pace of life slowed, but the need to make something for dinner quickly became essential – recipes that took minimal time, were comforting, but most of all delicious. So that's where this book comes in. *Balli Balli* translates as 'quickly, quickly,' and is something that we often say in Korea as we're usually in a hurry. Yet it's more than just a saying, it's a real Korean value and way of life, so when I was thinking of a title for this book, it seemed like the perfect fit.

You could think of *Balli Balli* as a simplified Korean cookbook, or a Korean cookbook with a twist. Recipes that use Korean flavours in a way that's easy, with minimal prep and a few shortcuts thrown in – because even though I'm feeling good now, I'm still mum to two highly energetic boys, so I need to be able to quickly whip up something tasty at dinner time!

When we were still living in London (close to the Korean hub of New Malden), we could go to our nearby Korean supermarket to get hold of pretty much any ingredient we needed. Now we live outside London, I just use the ingredients that I can easily get with my weekly shop, with an occasional run to the Asian store for extra items. I'm hoping this means that it'll be easy for you to recreate the recipes in this book, and that these recipes become part of your midweek staples.

INGREDIENTS

THE JANGS

'Jang' refers to fermented soybean products, with the most common being:

GOCHUJANG

A thick, sticky bright red paste, which is spicy, salty and sweet but has an earthiness and umami that comes from the fermented soy beans. It's incredibly versatile – in Korean cooking, it is often mixed with vinegar for a tangy dipping sauce, with *doenjang* for a seasoning paste for *ssam* (lettuce wraps) or with soy sauce and honey to make a deliciously addictive marinade. It can add a spicy kick to mayonnaise or a spoonful can provide a little heat to any other dish – I've known people use it as their secret ingredient in a huge range of dishes from curries to bolognese! It is usually found in a red tub.

DOENJANG

Doenjang is fermented soy bean paste, usually found in a brown tub – and I often describe it as miso's cousin. Although they share similarities, *doenjang* is much chunkier, saltier and intense in flavour. It's often used in soup, marinades and dipping sauces, but it can also be used as a seasoning for extra saltiness and to add depth.

GANJANG

Korean soy sauce can be split into two types – a regular soy sauce, which has a slightly caramel flavour, and light soy sauce, *guk ganjang*, which is thinner and saltier. The regular soy sauce is used most often in dipping sauces, marinades and braises. If you can't find Korean soy sauce, a Japanese alternative like Kikkoman is the most similar in flavour. The light soy sauce is used to season soups and vegetable dishes – and is a great vegan substitute for fish sauce when extra saltiness is needed.

THE PANTRY

In addition to the 'jangs', I also always keep the following in my pantry:

TOASTED SESAME SEEDS

I buy my sesame seeds already toasted, but if I can only find the untoasted ones, I always toast them myself first. To do this, place a large, dry pan on a medium heat with the sesame seeds. Heat the seeds for 1–2 minutes, stirring occasionally until they are lightly golden. Leave to cool completely before transferring to an airtight container. This way you can get the full flavour of the seeds.

TOASTED SESAME OIL

Similarly, the nutty aroma of toasted sesame oil is essential to Korean cooking. Blended sesame oils do not have the same level of flavour and it means that too much can be used which makes food greasy, so it is always worth using a 100% pure roasted sesame oil, where a little goes a long way.

GOCHUGARU

Korean red pepper flakes come in two types – coarse or fine. Coarse flakes are most common and are the type you're likely to need in your kitchen, as they're used for kimchis, marinades, braises – anything that needs a little heat. In Korean cooking, we add *gochujang* when we need saltiness, depth and spice combined – whereas *gochugaru* is used when only extra spice is needed. The very fine powder is used when making *gochujang* and is less commonly available.

NOODLES

I usually have a stash of noodles at home, which always include: bouncy udon noodles, *somyun* thin wheat noodles, slippery sweet potato *dangmyun* noodles and of course Korean *ramyun* instant noodles.

steamed rice. Freshly cooked rice is so fragrant and comforting to me, but it's not always possible to make when you're in a hurry – so I usually cook a big batch, let it cool completely, then freeze it in individual portions. On the days that I need rice in a hurry, I defrost these frozen portions in the microwave for a few minutes with a little splash of water.

FRESH & FROZEN

These fresh and frozen ingredients are staples in my kitchen:

KIMCHI

Kimchi is made from salted, fermented vegetables, which is eaten as a *banchan* (side dish) with almost every Korean meal. There are hundreds of different types, but the most common is the cabbage kimchi made using Chinese leaves. As well as a side dish, kimchi is an important ingredient in Korean cooking, and it is this cabbage kimchi that is used when it is mature, tangy and full of flavour.

GARLIC & GINGER

I keep ginger whole and in the freezer. It's not necessary to peel it – I just use a microplane to grate the quantity I need and this way there's always fresh ginger available. Similarly, I use a microplane to

The ones I use most often are the thin *somyun* noodles but these can be easily swapped for soba (buckwheat) noodles or thin, dried udon noodles, which are more commonly available in your local big supermarket.

RICE

Rice is so important to Korean people, that the word *bap* for rice is the same as the word for food.

Often, when Korean people eat a big meal that doesn't include rice, they feel like there is still a void in their stomachs that can only be filled with a bowl of rice. In Korea, we eat short grain (sushi) rice, which is white, sticky and shiny. Almost every meal is served with an individual bowl of rice and throughout this book, it is recommended that most of the dishes are served with freshly quickly grate a clove or two of garlic when needed. Sometimes I will peel a big batch and whizz it in the blender. Once puréed, the garlic can be put in a freezer bag, flattened out, then whenever I need some garlic (most of the recipes in this book do), I can just break a piece off. It's best to use fresh or frozen garlic and ginger over jarred, which is usually preserved in oil or vinegar and can change the flavour of a dish.

SPRING ONIONS/SCALLIONS

These are great for cooking with, can be snipped with a pair of scissors (so no need for a chopping board) and add a lovely freshness when scattered over a dish.

RICE CAKES

Rice cakes can be found in the ambient, chilled and frozen sections of large Asian supermarkets, but the chilled ones generally have the best chewy texture. They come in either thin oval-shaped slices or long cylinders (*garae tteok*). If using frozen, they need to be pre-soaked before cooking for 20 minutes to soften.

FROZEN FISHCAKES

Korean fishcakes sometimes borrow the Japanese word *odeng* but are also called *eomuk* in Korean. They make a great *banchan* (side dish) when stir-fried with

a little soy sauce and chilli/chile, can be added to soups and are often eaten alongside *tteokbokki*.

FROZEN MANDU

Mandu (Korean dumplings) are available at the big supermarkets

now – but can also be substituted for frozen gyoza (which are even easier to get hold of). They're really handy to keep in the freezer, as they can be added to soups and instant noodles straight from the freezer for a filling speedy meal.

KIMCHI, PICKLES & SIDES

김치, 장아찌, 반찬

BANCHAN ARE OFTEN DESCRIBED AS 'SIDE DISHES', AS THEY ARE THE SELECTION OF SMALL PLATES THAT ARE SERVED IN THE MIDDLE OF THE TABLE TO SHARE. When you order food at a restaurant in Korea – whether it's a big Korean BBQ or a simple soup – a selection of *banchan* are usually given as *service* (for free) as part of the meal. These *banchan* might include *namul* (seasoned vegetables), kimchi and pickles – as well as braised meats, marinated eggs or even grilled fish. The thing that makes *banchan* more than just side dishes though, is the fact that in most Korean households, there are always a few staple *banchan* in the fridge, so that when pulled together with a bowl of rice, there's a quick meal ready, and these can be enjoyed in various combinations for breakfast, lunch and dinner.

Kimchi and pickles were born out of the need to preserve vegetables, so by design they are the perfect *banchan* to have handy in the fridge as they last for such a long time. It's a tradition in Korea that families, friends and local communities get together to make big batches of kimchi in November for *kimjang* (collective kimchi making), when cabbages are at their best. This *kimchi* lasts throughout the harsh winter months and becomes fuller in flavour as it matures. When ripened, it's called *mugeunji* kimchi, and is the best for cooking in soups, stews and braises.

Nowadays, the combination of busy lives and city living mean that *kimjang* is less common than it used to be, but fortunately in Korea, kimchi is easy to buy. In the UK, kimchi is easier to get hold of than it used to be, but it varies in quality. Avoid kimchi from the ambient aisles of the supermarket – they tend to not taste particularly authentic – and if possible, always buy the refrigerated ones. Alternatively, make a big batch of the *mak kimchi* (see page 16) so that you always have kimchi on hand – it's an important ingredient in so much Korean cooking (fried rice, noodles, dumplings to name a few) and adds a great flavour boost to any dish. It's definitely worth the time investment, because it tastes much better than the shop-bought variety and is much more cost effective.

I always have kimchi in the fridge and make a few other *banchan* throughout the week, which means that it's always easy to pull together something delicious and nutritious in a hurry. Any *banchan* can be mixed together with rice, a dollop of *gochujang* (Korean red pepper paste) and sesame oil to create a delicious *bibimbap* (mixed rice) for a speedy lunch, eaten simply as sides with a bowl of freshly steamed rice or served alongside a main dish as part of a larger meal – it really is meal prep at its finest.

QUICK CUT KIMCHI

Cabbage kimchi is usually made in one of two ways. For *poggi* (whole cabbage kimchi), the cabbage is cut in half (sometimes into quarters), vertically down the middle, with the leaves remaining intact with the stalk. The cabbage is then brined and each leaf is stuffed and coated with the spicy kimchi paste. This is really the best way to make kimchi as it benefits from a slower fermentation process. The end result is deliciously crisp kimchi with the added bonus of being able to enjoy eating the combination of the crunchy base of the cabbage along with the leafy tops, which take on all the flavour of the paste.

However, making *mak* (cut cabbage) kimchi is much quicker. There's less waiting time for the brining and also means that you have ready cut kimchi to hand for when you need it as an ingredient for Kimchi Pancakes (see page 45), Mandu Crisps and Kimchi Salsa (see page 50), Kimchi and Bacon Fried Rice (see page 126), or a million other things you can cook with kimchi.

1 Chinese cabbage
   (about 600 g/1 lb. 5 oz.)
3 tbsp sea salt flakes
1 tbsp crushed/minced garlic
1 tbsp crushed/minced fresh ginger
1 apple, cored and finely sliced
   (peel on)
3 tbsp *gochugaru*
   (Korean red pepper flakes)
4 tbsp fish sauce

1-litre/4-cup jar or container

MAKES 1 LARGE JAR

Cut the cabbage into bite-sized pieces, wash thoroughly and drain. Place the cabbage into a large bowl with the salt. Using your hands, mix the salt into the cabbage and set to one side for 30 minutes. Mix again and leave to brine for another 30 minutes.

Rinse the cabbage thoroughly under cold water, drain and shake off the excess water.

Place the cabbage back into the large bowl, along with the remaining kimchi ingredients. Using your hands (wearing gloves!), make sure to thoroughly mix all the ingredients together.

Transfer the kimchi into a large jar or clip-lock airtight container. Press down across the top, wipe away any excess paste, then close the lid.

Leave at room temperature for 3 days, then transfer to the fridge. The kimchi will take on its distinctive sour flavour after about 2 weeks.

CHILLED WATER KIMCHI

나박 김치

NABAK KIMCHI

Nabak kimchi is a water kimchi – one with lots of tangy liquid that is best when served really cold. It's a fantastic one for the summer, as the tart kimchi is the perfect side dish to balance out any barbecued meats, and the liquid can also be used as a chilled broth for noodles. Simply put some cooked, rinsed noodles in a bowl and ladle the kimchi with plenty of liquid on top for instantly cooling, refreshing noodles – great to beat the summer heat.

300 g/10½ oz. mooli, peeled

1 Chinese cabbage
   (about 600 g/1 lb. 5 oz.),
   cut into bite-sized pieces

3½ tbsp fish sauce

2½ tbsp sea salt flakes

1 tbsp *gochugaru*
   (Korean red pepper flakes)

3 spring onions/scallions,
   cut into thirds

3 garlic cloves, finely sliced

2 long red chillies/chiles,
   finely sliced

1 pear, peeled, cored and
   cut into thin slices

½ onion, finely sliced

1 tbsp caster/granulated sugar

2-litre/quart airtight container
muslin or clean tea/dish towel

MAKES A 2-LITRE/QUART CONTAINER

Cut the mooli into quarters lengthways and then into thin slices, about 5-mm/¼-inch thick.

Place the mooli in a large bowl with the cabbage and mix in the fish sauce and salt. Set aside for 20 minutes.

Pour 2 litres/quarts water into the bowl with the cabbage and mooli (no need to rinse it first).

Spoon the *gochugaru* into a small square of muslin or a clean tea/dish towel and make a little parcel. Squeeze the muslin parcel into the water to release the colour from the *gochugaru* until it turns a light pink. Discard the parcel, then add all the remaining ingredients to the bowl and mix.

Transfer to the airtight container with the lid on. Leave at room temperature for 2 days, then transfer to the fridge. The kimchi is ready to eat after 4–5 days when it starts to taste tangy and fresh.

SPEEDY MOOLI KIMCHI

When we first moved to England, it was difficult to get hold of Korean ingredients in the UK, and it took a while for my mum to work out how to replicate the flavours of home. *Kkakduggi* is a crunchy kimchi, usually made from *moo* (Korean radish), which has a much higher water content than the more commonly available mooli. When my mum and her Korean friends tried to make kimchi the traditional way but with mooli, they found that it was much drier so it didn't need the brine that would usually draw out excess water from the *moo*, and so, this simpler kimchi was born! You can also substitute the mooli for turnip or swede, which is equally delicious and is a kimchi we still often have now.

1 mooli (750 g/1 lb. 10 oz.), peeled and cut into 1-cm/½-inch cubes
1 apple, left unpeeled, cored and roughly cut
3 garlic cloves
15 g/½ oz. piece of fresh ginger
1½ tbsp cooked rice
8 tbsp *gochugaru* (Korean red pepper flakes)
8 tbsp fish sauce

MAKES 1 LITRE/4 CUPS

Place the mooli in a large mixing bowl.

Put all the rest of the ingredients in a blender and whizz into a smooth paste. Scrape the mixture into the bowl with the mooli. Using your hands (wearing gloves!), mix the mooli into the paste, making sure everything is completely coated.

Transfer all the kimchi into an airtight container or large jar, making sure to press down and smooth out the top. Clean the edges of the container with paper towel to remove any excess kimchi paste and close the lid.

Leave to ferment at room temperature for 3 days before transferring to the fridge. Best eaten after 1–2 weeks, when the kimchi becomes sour from fermentation.

TIP *Traditionally, a rice glue is made using glutinous rice flour, which is heated in a pan with water, then left to cool down. This is a quicker version using any leftover cooked rice or even microwave rice so that you don't have to wait.*

CHIVE KIMCHI

In Korea, garlic chives are very affordable. You can buy huge bags of them to make big batches of delicious *buchu* (garlic chive) kimchi. It's the easiest kimchi to make as there's no brining and no chopping (garlic isn't even needed as the chives have plenty of their own flavour), so it's simply a case of mixing the (very few) ingredients together. It is undoubtedly my mum's favourite kimchi and it is great eaten as a *banchan* side dish, but even better as an ingredient in *bibimbap* (mixed rice), where you stir it into warm rice with whatever *namul* (seasoned vegetables) you have in the fridge, some sesame oil and *gochujang* (Korean red pepper paste).

100 g/3½ oz. chives
3 tbsp fish sauce
3 tbsp *gochugaru*
   (Korean red pepper flakes)
1 tbsp granulated sugar

MAKES 370-G/13 OZ. JAR

In a large bowl, mix all the ingredients together using your hands (wearing gloves!). Transfer to a jar or airtight container, pressing down on the top with a spoon to submerge the chives.

This kimchi can be enjoyed immediately or is even more delicious after a few days in the fridge.

TIP *In this recipe, I have used the more commonly available (onion) chives, but if you can get hold of garlic chives, please use these instead for an even stronger flavour.*

SOY MARINATED EGGS

GYERAN JJANGAJJI

These eggs are sometimes also called *mayak gyeran* or 'drug eggs' as they're so moreish, but I've been convinced by my mum to use a less divisive name here! They are such a great *banchan* side dish to have handy in the fridge. You can keep them chilled for 3–4 days, and each day they will get a little darker and saltier as they absorb the marinade. I love them served simply over a bowl of freshly steamed rice with a spoonful of the soy sauce marinade, a little splash of sesame oil and a sprinkle of sesame seeds on top for a quick lunch, but they also make a great addition to a bowl of noodles or salad. The recipe below is for eggs with a jammy yolk (my favourite), but add an extra minute or two to the boiling time if you like your centres more set.

6 medium eggs
250 ml/1 cup Korean soy sauce
3½ tbsp caster/granulated sugar
2 spring onions/scallions, finely chopped
2 long red chillies/chiles, finely chopped
1 tsp crushed/minced garlic

MAKES 6

Place a medium saucepan of water over a high heat and bring to the boil. Once boiling, gently add the eggs and boil for 6 minutes (7–8 minutes if you like them less soft).

Meanwhile, place all the remaining ingredients in an airtight container or large jar with 250 ml/1 cup water.

Once the eggs are ready, carefully take them out of the pan and plunge into a bowl of ice water.

Peel the eggs and put them in the container of soy sauce, making sure they are properly submerged, then close the lid.

Leave for at least 1 hour to absorb the soy sauce flavour before eating.

양파 장아찌
YANGPA JJANGAJJI

무생채
MUSAENGCHAE

SOY PICKLED ONIONS

QUICK MOOLI SIDE DISH

It's always handy to have some pickles in the fridge and this is the one that I make the most often. These add a great salty, tangy flavour to a *ssam* (lettuce wrap), as a side to a barbecue or as a *banchan* (side dish) to any Korean meal. *Jjangajji* means 'soy pickled vegetables' in Korean, and you can use the same pickling liquid for any vegetables. We go foraging for wild garlic each year and if you're lucky to come across some, I would definitely recommend pickling them in this way too.

This spicy, crunchy *banchan* (side dish) is often used as a topping for *bibimbap* (mixed rice). It is a great one to have in the fridge because you can eat it straight away, but if you leave it for a few days, it will take on the tangy, slightly sour flavour of fermented kimchi as it matures.

500 g/1 lb. 2 oz. mooli, peeled
   and cut into matchsticks
1 tbsp salt
1 tbsp caster/granulated sugar
1½ tbsp *gochugaru*
   (Korean red pepper flakes)
2 tbsp rice wine vinegar
1 tsp crushed/minced garlic

SERVES 4 AS A BANCHAN

4 tbsp caster/granulated sugar
100 ml/scant ½ cup Korean
   apple/rice vinegar
100 ml/scant ½ cup Korean
   soy sauce
2 onions, chopped into
   2.5-cm/1-inch squares

SERVES 4–6 AS A BANCHAN

Mix the mooli with the salt and leave for 10 minutes. Rinse thoroughly and squeeze out any excess water. Mix in the remaining ingredients and serve. Store in the fridge and use within 5 days.

Mix the sugar, vinegar, soy sauce and 50 ml/scant ¼ cup water together in a bowl.

Place the onions in a sterilized jar and pour the liquid over the top so that they are fully submerged.

These can be eaten straight away but are really best enjoyed the next day when the flavours have soaked into the onions. Use within 2 weeks.

BAECHU DOENJANG MUCHIM

HOBAK NAMUL

CHINESE LEAVES WITH KOREAN SOY BEAN DRESSING

Dressed in a *doenjang* (Korean soy bean paste) sauce, these Chinese leaves are a light *banchan* (side dish) full of nutty, earthy flavours.

300 g/10½ oz. Chinese leaves
   (or pak choi/bok choy)
1 tsp salt
1 tbsp *doenjang*
   (Korean soy bean paste)
1½ tsp crushed/minced garlic
1½ tbsp toasted sesame oil
1 tbsp toasted sesame seeds,
   plus extra to garnish
1 tsp *gochugaru*
   (Korean red pepper flakes)

SERVES 4 AS A BANCHAN

Trim and separate the Chinese leaves and wash them thoroughly.

Bring a saucepan of water to the boil with the salt. Add the Chinese leaves and blanch for about 3–4 minutes until soft. Drain and rinse under cold water, squeezing out any excess.

Cut the cabbage into bite-sized pieces, then place in a bowl, along with the remaining ingredients and mix thoroughly by hand.

Serve topped with extra sesame seeds.

STIR-FRIED COURGETTE WITH CHILLI

We always have courgettes/zucchini in our fridge as we use them in so many dishes – from *jjigae* (stews), to *yache jeon* (vegetable pancakes), to this stir-fried *banchan* (side dish). The secret to making these courgettes extra tasty is to salt them first, which not only seasons them properly, but also maintains a firmer texture so they hold their shape.

1 courgette/zucchini,
   cut into 5-mm/¼-inch slices
1 tsp sea salt flakes
1 tbsp vegetable oil
½ red chilli/chile, finely sliced
½ spring onion/scallion, finely sliced
1 tbsp toasted sesame seeds
1 tbsp toasted sesame oil
1 tsp crushed/minced garlic
½ tsp fish sauce
pinch of ground white pepper

SERVES 4 AS A BANCHAN

Place the courgettes into a bowl with the salt, mix and set to one side for 10 minutes. Drain the courgettes of any excess water.

Place a frying pan/skillet over a medium heat with the vegetable oil. Add the courgettes and fry for 1–2 minutes, then add the remaining ingredients. Fry for a further 1–2 minutes until the courgettes have slightly softened. This can be served both hot and cold.

된장 고추 무침
DOENJANG GOCHU MUCHIM

CHILLIES IN SOY BEAN SAUCE

As well as making lots of her own *banchan*, growing up my mum would often make the journey to New Malden (the Korean hub in London) to stock up on extra pre-prepared *banchan* to fill our fridge. One of my favourites was chillies/chiles in a *doenjang* (soy bean paste) sauce. I've always loved chillies, and together with the *doenjang*, it makes for a really simple side dish. Soaking the chillies first takes away some of the fiery heat so that they have a more subtle spice that's perfect for a *ssam* (lettuce wrap).

10 long red chillies/chiles,
    chopped into 1-cm/½-inch pieces
1½ tbsp *doenjang*
    (Korean soy bean paste)
1 tbsp toasted sesame oil
1 tbsp honey
1 tbsp toasted sesame seeds
½ tsp crushed/minced garlic

SERVES 4 AS A BANCHAN

Place the chillies in a medium-sized bowl with enough water to cover and leave for 5 minutes.

Meanwhile, mix the remaining ingredients together in a small bowl.

Drain the chillies and shake them to remove any excess water, then stir in the sauce.

These can be eaten immediately, but are best enjoyed the next day once the flavours have had some extra time to absorb. Store in the fridge and use within 3 days.

브로콜리 무침
BROCCOLI MUCHIM

GARLIC SESAME BROCCOLI

I often season steamed or blanched vegetables with sesame oil and garlic. It's such a simple way of making vegetables taste more interesting. It's also easy to make several quick *banchan* (side dishes) as you can dress lots of different vegetables this way and still get a lovely mixture of colours and flavours on the dinner table.

200 g/7 oz. Tenderstem
    broccoli/broccolini
pinch of salt
1 tbsp toasted sesame seeds
1½ tsp toasted sesame oil
1 tsp light soy sauce
¼ tsp crushed/minced garlic

SERVES 2-4 AS A BANCHAN

Trim the ends of the broccoli and cut any thicker stems in half so that they are all of even thickness.

Place a saucepan of water over a high heat, add a pinch of salt and bring to the boil.

Once boiling, add the broccoli and cook for about 3-4 minutes until tender enough to pierce the stems easily with a fork. Drain and shake off any excess water.

Place the remaining ingredients in a medium bowl and mix together. Add the broccoli and toss to make sure that each piece is coated in the dressing.

SPICY FISH CAKES

어묵 볶음

EOMUK BOKKEUM

This is one of my favourite *banchan* (side dishes) and it was one of the staples in our fridge when I was little. As well as a *banchan*, I love eating this as a *kimbap* (seaweed roll) by taking a seaweed sheet, adding a thin layer of rice and using the *eomuk bokkeum* as a spicy filling. *Kimbap* filled with spicy *eomuk* is always my go-to order at the train station when I travel from Seoul to Busan, but it's also so easy to recreate at home.

1 tbsp vegetable oil
250 g/9 oz. frozen *eomuk/odeng* (Korean fish cakes), defrosted and cut into bite-sized pieces
½ carrot, finely sliced
1 onion, finely sliced
2 spring onions/scallions, roughly chopped
1 long red chilli/chile, finely sliced
1 tbsp toasted sesame seeds

SAUCE
1½ tbsp *gochujang* (Korean red pepper paste)
1½ tbsp *gochugaru* (Korean red pepper flakes)
2 tbsp honey
1 tbsp mirin
1 tbsp Korean soy sauce
1½ tsp crushed/minced garlic
¼ tsp ground white pepper

SERVES 4 AS A BANCHAN

Mix the sauce ingredients with 3 tablespoons water in a small bowl and set to one side.

Place a large frying pan/skillet over a medium heat with the vegetable oil. Add the fish cakes, carrot and onion and fry for 3–4 minutes until the fish cakes are lightly browned and the carrots have softened.

Stir in the sauce, the spring onion and chilli. Keep stirring for 2 minutes until the sauce is reduced and sticky. Stir in the sesame seeds to finish.

SWEET SOY POTATOES

감자 조림
GAMJA JORIM

These potatoes are a popular *banchan* (side dish) in Korea. They are so easy and delicious that they're sure to be a favourite in your house too. You don't even have to cut the potatoes – leave them whole if you're in a hurry (just increase the cooking time until you can pierce them with a fork), but I like to cut them so that the sweet soy sauce can really cling to them and the edges brown nicely in the pan, making them extra tasty.

500 g/1 lb. 2 oz. baby/
   new potatoes, cut in half
4 tbsp Korean soy sauce
2 tbsp light soft brown sugar
2 tsp crushed/minced garlic
1½ tbsp vegetable oil

TO GARNISH
1 tbsp toasted sesame seeds
   (optional)
1 spring onion/scallion,
   finely sliced

SERVES 2–4 AS A BANCHAN

Place a large saucepan filled with water over a high heat. Add the potatoes and bring to the boil. Cook for 12–15 minutes until tender enough to insert a fork, then drain.

Meanwhile, mix together the soy sauce, sugar, garlic and 3 tablespoons water in a small bowl.

Place a large frying pan/skillet over a medium heat with the oil. Add the potatoes and fry for 5 minutes until nicely golden.

Pour the sauce over the potatoes and reduce the heat to low. Use a pair of tongs to make sure the potatoes are coated in the sauce. Simmer for 2 minutes until the sauce has thickened and becomes sticky.

Stir in the sesame seeds, if using, and spring onions and serve. This can be eaten hot or cold.

LUNCHBOX
& STREET
FOOD

도시락,
포장마차

IN KOREA, STREET FOOD IS EVERYWHERE – from the individual carts that pop up on a street corner, to markets packed full of stalls that are a real sensory experience with the noise, the smells, the delicious food and the bustling atmosphere. Gwangjang market in Seoul is probably the most famous street-food area as it has appeared on so many TV shows, but my favourite place to go for street food in Korea is in Nampodong in Busan. This area is lined with street-food carts, marked with their distinctive red parasols, that sell a huge variety of treats, including *ojingeo* (dried squid), *soondae* (Korean blood sausage), *odeng* (fish cakes), *buchu jeon* (chive pancakes), and my favourites, *tteokbokki* (spicy rice cakes), which are particularly spicy in Busan. You'll also fine *hotteok*, which are doughy filled pancakes and usually filled with a cinnamon sugar mixture, but in Busan they add seeds too, lending a delicious nuttiness to the oozy melted brown sugar inside.

When I think about the food I crave most in Korea, it's these street foods. I have so many great memories of huddling around these street-food carts, eating until I simply couldn't fit in any more. The food is always packed full of flavour and it's so much fun to go from cart to cart sampling all the different dishes. Some street-food areas only open at night, which my kids love as it really adds to the atmosphere and excitement of it all. Their highlight of our most recent trip was going to Bupyeong Kkangton Market, which sells all sorts of wares from clothes and accessories to electronics during the day, but then shuts in the evening when a huge line of street-food vendors open and stretch down the length of the market. If you ever get to visit Korea, make the most of the glittering evenings as 'Korea really comes alive at night' (as my eldest says).

One street food that you can always get, whether day or night, is *kimbap* (seaweed rolls), filled with rice and lots of cooked fillings and seasoned with sesame oil. I always think of it as a Korean sandwich, as the rice and seaweed are really a vehicle for whatever filling you want to put inside – they can be anything from hot dogs, tuna, vegetables or any leftover cooked meat. As they're so portable, *kimbap* are often eaten at picnics, taken on hiking trips and are common in lunchboxes, which made me think of what else we usually have in Korea in a packed lunch. This section of the book covers a few ideas for tasty alternatives to a sandwich that can be eaten hot or cold and are perfect to take on your next picnic or office lunch.

ADDICTIVE SEAWEED ROLLS

Traditionally, these were often called *mayak kimbap* with *mayak* translating as 'drugs' due to their addictive nature, particularly when eaten with the tangy, nutty, sesame mustard sauce. However, they're also called *goma kimbap* with *goma* translating as 'toddler', which sounds much nicer and is also perfectly fitting as they are mini (toddler sized) and particularly great for little hands. They are easy and fun to make and are a great alternative to a sandwich for a picnic.

150 g/1 generous cup freshly cooked sushi rice
4 tsp toasted sesame oil
¼ tsp salt
75 g/1½ cups spinach
1 tsp toasted sesame seeds, plus extra to garnish
½ tbsp vegetable oil
1 carrot, peeled and julienned
3 sheets gim/nori (sushi seaweed)
100 g/3½ oz. *danmuji* (Korean yellow pickled radish), cut into 1-cm/½-inch thick strips (or use sliced gherkins/pickled cucumbers)
salt

SESAME MUSTARD SAUCE
1 tbsp toasted sesame seeds
1 tbsp Korean soy sauce
1 tbsp Korean apple/rice vinegar
2 tsp caster/granulated sugar
1½ tsp English mustard

MAKES 10 SEAWEED ROLLS

Make the mustard sauce first. Crush the sesame seeds in a mortar and then mix in the remaining ingredients. Pour the sauce into a dipping bowl and set to one side until needed.

Mix the cooked sushi rice with 2 teaspoons of the sesame oil and the salt and set to one side.

Place the spinach in a bowl and cover with boiling water to blanch. Leave for 2 minutes, then drain and squeeze out any excess. Mix with the remaining sesame oil and the sesame seeds, then set to one side.

Place a frying pan/skillet over a medium heat with the vegetable oil. Fry the carrot for 1–2 minutes with a pinch of salt until just cooked and slightly softened. Set to one side.

Cut a sheet of seaweed into quarters. Place it shiny side down and spread a thin, even layer of rice over the top. Lay the prepared vegetables on top of the bottom third of the rice-covered seaweed (closest to you).

Lift the entire bottom edge with both hands and roll it over the filling away from you, tucking in the filling with your fingers. Place firm pressure over the roll to close everything in tightly. Then, continue to roll again, using pressure evenly over the roll with both hands.

Use a few grains of cooked rice as glue to seal the *kimbap* closed. Rub or brush the top of the *kimbap* with a little bit of sesame oil for extra flavour and shine. Repeat the process to make 10 mini *kimbap*.

Sprinkle some sesame seeds on the top for decoration and serve with the mustard dipping sauce.

FISH CAKE SOUP

Tteokbokki (spicy rice cakes) are the food that I crave the most from Korea, but it's the combination of having them with these *eomuk* (fish cakes) that makes them really special. In Korea, these two street foods go hand in hand and *tteokbokki* street-food sellers usually have a big rectangular pot of *eomuk* bubbling away too, and you help yourself to cups of the broth as you eat the *tteokbokki*. The *eomuk* sold at the *pojangmachas* (street-food tents) are usually threaded onto long skewers (like in this picture). Ready-skewered *eomuk* can be found in the frozen section in some stores, but the sheets of fish cake are usually more easily available, so I've cut them into bite-sized pieces in this recipe to make things quick and easy.

150 g/5½ oz. mooli, cut into half moons around 5-mm/¼-inch thick
2 garlic cloves, finely sliced
2 tbsp Korean soy sauce
2½ tbsp fish sauce
300 g/10½ oz. *eomuk* (Korean fish cakes), cut into 2-cm/¾-inch squares
2 spring onions/scallions, roughly chopped

SAUCE
4 tbsp Korean soy sauce
1 spring onion/scallion, finely chopped
¼ onion, roughly chopped
¼ tsp crushed/minced garlic

SERVES 2

Mix together the sauce ingredients with 2 tablespoons water in a small bowl and set to one side.

Fill a medium saucepan with 1 litre/4 cups water and bring to the boil over a high heat.

Once boiling, add the mooli, garlic, soy sauce, fish sauce and continue cooking for 3 minutes. Add the *eomuk* and spring onions and boil for a further 2 minutes.

Serve with the sauce on the side and dip the *eomuk* pieces into the sauce to season.

TIP *Make this alongside* tteokbokki *(spicy rice cakes, page 42) for an authentic Korean experience, or simply serve with a bowl of steamed rice.*

SPICY STREET FOOD RICE CAKES

떡볶이
TTEOKBOKKI

Tteokbokki are my absolute favourite street food and I'm always really excited to eat them whenever I go to Korea. There's something pretty special about huddling around a street-food cart with all the amazing smells, eating *tteokbokki* off a plastic plate (for minimal washing up for the vendor) and drinking paper cups full of *eomuk tang* broth (see page 41), which is the perfect pairing to this spicy dish.

Although I can't quite recreate the scene here in the UK, *tteokbokki* is very easy to make so I really hope you give this a go (along with the *eomuk tang*/fish cake soup for the full experience) so you can try these delightfully chewy, spicy rice cakes at home.

500 g/1 lb. 2 oz. *garae tteok*
   (long Korean rice cakes)
200 g/7 oz. frozen *eomuk/odeng*
   (Korean fish cake sheets),
   cut into bite-sized pieces
2 spring onions/scallions,
   roughly chopped

SAUCE
2 tbsp *gochujang*
   (Korean red pepper paste)
2 tbsp Korean soy sauce
3½ tbsp caster/granulated sugar
1 tbsp corn syrup (see tip)

SERVES 3–4

Mix the sauce ingredients together in a small bowl.

Place a large frying pan/skillet over a high heat with 500 ml/2 cups water and bring to the boil. Add the sauce, along with the rice cakes and fish cakes and stir together.

Continue to boil for 10–12 minutes until the rice cakes are soft and the sauce has thickened, stirring occasionally to make sure the rice cakes don't stick to the bottom of the pan.

Stir in the spring onions (saving some of the green part to sprinkle over at the end) and simmer for a further minute until the spring onion softens. Serve immediately.

TIP *Corn syrup gives this dish its signature glossiness, but this can be replaced with honey or golden syrup instead if you prefer.*

KIMCHI PANCAKE

김치전

KIMCHI JEON

There's something so addictive about *kimchi jeon*. Out of all the *jeons* (savoury pancakes), it is definitely one of my favourites and the smell of it crisping up in the pan just makes my mouth water. It can be found all over Korea as a street food, a *banchan* (side dish), but most commonly as an *anju*. *Anju* are foods that you share while drinking alcohol, and the salty, spicy, savoury flavours of *kimchi jeon* really work perfectly for this. It is the best pairing for *makgeolli* (Korean rice wine), *soju* (Korean spirit) or even a cold glass of beer.

200 g/1½ cups plain/all-purpose
  flour
1½ tsp baking powder
3 tbsp cornflour/cornstarch
200 g/7 oz. fermented (sour)
  kimchi, drained and finely
  chopped
1 tsp *gochujang*
  (Korean red pepper paste)
2 spring onions/scallions,
  finely sliced, plus extra to garnish
vegetable oil, for frying

DIPPING SAUCE (OPTIONAL)
½ long green chilli/chile, finely
  chopped
1 tbsp Korean apple/rice vinegar
2 tbsp Korean soy sauce
pinch of toasted sesame seeds

**MAKES 2 LARGE PANCAKES
(SERVES 2–4)**

Place the flour in the bowl and add 200 ml/scant 1 cup cold water. Whisk until a smooth batter is formed. Mix in the remaining ingredients, except the oil – the batter should be a slightly thick pancake batter.

Place a large, non-stick frying pan/skillet over a high heat with 2 tablespoons vegetable oil.

Ladle half of the pancake mix into the pan. Use the back of the ladle to smooth the mixture out to create a thin, even layer. Reduce the heat to medium-high and fry for 2–3 minutes until air bubbles start to pop on the surface and the sides start to crisp.

Flip the pancake. Slightly lift the side of the pancake with a spatula and add another tablespoon of oil underneath – shake the pan a little to make sure the oil coats the bottom of the pancake. Use the spatula to press on top of the pancake to ensure the pancake is thin and crispy.

Fry for a further 2 minutes. Flip one last time, pressing down on the pancake again and fry for 30 seconds. Drain on paper towels and repeat with the remaining batter to make a second pancake.

Mix the dipping sauce ingredients together in a small bowl, if using.

Cut the pancakes into bite-sized pieces and serve immediately, garnished with spring onions, with the dipping sauce alongside.

TIP *For extra flavour and colour, replace 2–3 tablespoons of the water in the batter with the drained kimchi juice.*

KIMCHI
HOTDOG

Hotdogs made their way to Korea via the American rations handed out during the Korean war, but have had a lasting impact. Today, mini frankfurters can often be seen as *banchan* (side dishes), corn dogs have become a popular Korean street food and frankfurters are often used as a filling in *kimbap* (seaweed rolls). The best Korean fusion, though, is when it is combined with kimchi as its acidity and spice contrasts with the smoky sausages to make the best hotdog ever. I also like to add a *gochujang* yogurt here for extra flavour. You could sub out the yogurt for sour cream or mayonnaise, but I don't love mayonnaise and I think the yogurt here makes a nicer, lighter alternative.

2 hot dog rolls
vegetable oil, for frying
2 frankfurter sausages
200 g/7 oz. kimchi, drained
  and roughly chopped
½ tsp *gochugaru*
  (Korean red pepper flakes)
¼ tsp granulated sugar

GOCHUJANG YOGURT
2 tbsp natural yogurt
1 tsp *gochujang*
  (Korean red pepper paste)
¼ tsp crushed/minced garlic

TO FINISH
American mustard
1 spring onion/scallion,
  finely chopped

MAKES 2 HOTDOGS

Slice along the top of each of the hot dog rolls lengthways.

Mix the *gochujang* yogurt ingredients together in a small bowl.

Place a large frying pan/skillet over a high heat and lightly grease with 1 teaspoon vegetable oil, then add the frankfurters. Heat through for 2 minutes, making sure to turn the frankfurters every 30 seconds so that they colour evenly, then set to one side.

Place the pan back over a high heat with 2 tablespoons vegetable oil. Add the kimchi and fry for 2 minutes. Add the *gochugaru* and sugar and fry for 1 minute.

Warm the hot dog rolls in the microwave for 20 seconds. Smear the inside of each roll with a tablespoon of the *gochujang* yoghurt. Add the frankfurter and top with the fried kimchi.

Finish with American mustard and chopped spring onions.

TIP *To make these hotdogs extra special, try topping with crispy shallots or bacon for added flavour.*

SOY-GLAZED CHICKEN SKEWERS

DAK GOTCHI

When my eldest was three, I took him on his first trip to Korea. We had such a fun-packed time, meeting up with cousins, going to the beach, riding the cable car in Songdo… but the one memory that really stuck in his head was eating the *dak gotchi* (chicken skewers) in Nampodong in Busan. I love this area for street food, and I'm not sure if it was because the chicken skewer he had was so big, or because he genuinely loved the taste, but whenever we spoke about his Korea trip afterwards, he would always speak about these chicken skewers with huge enthusiasm, so I had to make these for him. Fortunately, he loves them just as much at home as he did on that trip.

6 spring onions/scallions

500 g/1 lb. 2 oz. boneless, skinless chicken thighs

¼ tsp salt

¼ tsp ground white pepper

1 tbsp vegetable oil

sliced red chilli/chile, to garnish (optional)

SAUCE

1 tbsp oyster sauce

2 tsp crushed/minced garlic

2 tbsp honey

¼ tsp ground white pepper

5–6 skewers (if using wooden skewers, soak them for 30 minutes in warm water first)

MAKES 5–6 SKEWERS

Put a saucepan over a medium-high heat. Add all the sauce ingredients along with 3 tablespoons water and simmer for 2 minutes until bubbling. Set to one side.

Cut the spring onions into 5-cm/2-inch lengths and the chicken into bite-sized pieces. Skewer in an alternating pattern on to 5–6 skewers.

Place a cast-iron pan (or large frying pan/skillet) over a medium-high heat and brush with oil. Lay the chicken skewers in the pan and brush with sauce. Cook for 3 minutes, then flip and brush with more sauce. Flip again, brush with sauce and cook for a further 3 minutes. Repeat once more and then serve immediately garnished with red chilli if liked.

TIP *These are also really delicious cooked in an air fryer. Set the air fryer to 190°C/375°F. Place the skewers on a tray and place on the highest shelf. Cook for 7 minutes on one side, flip them over and cook for a further 7 minutes. Brush with the sauce, cook for 3 minutes, flip and brush with more sauce and cook for a further 3 minutes.*

MANDU CRISPS & KIMCHI SALSA

만두칩 김치 살사

MANDU CHIP KIMCHI SALSA

Did you know that if you drop dumpling skins into a pan of hot oil, they puff up and turn into deliciously crunchy crisps/chips? Back in the days when we had our food truck, Busan BBQ, we used to also 'pop up' in restaurants across London. One of our pop ups was at Unwined, a fantastic wine shop in Tooting Market, where the lovely Laura and Kiki paired their wines with a selection of Korean-inspired dishes, which ranged from nibbles to big plates. One of the 'nibbles' we served back then were these dumpling crisps with kimchi salsa. These are the perfect sharing snack – a great *anju* (snack to serve with drinks) – and the kimchi salsa is also a delicious topping to the Korean Smashed Tacos (see page 75).

KIMCHI SALSA
150 g/5½ oz. tomatoes
½ tsp salt
125 g/4½ oz. kimchi, drained and finely chopped
¼ red onion, finely chopped
1 spring onion/scallion, finely chopped
½ long red chilli/chile, finely chopped
juice of ½ lime
2 tsp *gochugaru* (Korean red pepper flakes)
½ tsp light brown soft sugar

MANDU CRISPS/CHIPS
125 g/4½ oz. *mandu* (or gyoza) dumpling skins (if using frozen, defrost overnight in the fridge before use)
½ tsp salt
vegetable oil, for frying

SERVES 4

First, make the salsa. Finely chop the tomatoes and place them in a bowl with ¼ teaspoon of the salt.

Place the kimchi, red onion, spring onion and chilli in a separate bowl. Squeeze in the lime juice and mix in the *gochugaru*, sugar and remaining salt. Drain any liquid from the tomatoes and add them to the rest of the salsa ingredients. Mix and set to one side.

Place a deep frying pan/skillet (or wok) over a high heat with enough oil to cover the bottom 5–6 cm/2–2½ inches deep. Heat to 180°C/350°F, or until you can drop a small bit of dumping skin into the oil and it sizzles and floats to the top.

Cut the dumpling skins into quarters and separate any that are stuck together. Carefully drop them into the oil, using a pair of heatproof tongs to prevent the skins from sticking to each other. This is best done in batches to make sure the dumpling skins have enough space.

Fry for 40 seconds, or until the dumpling skins float and the edges start to colour. Remove from the pan and place the cooked dumpling crisps onto a plate lined with paper towels to drain.

Season generously with salt and serve with the kimchi salsa.

50 LUNCHBOX & STREET FOOD

CRISPY VEGETABLE PANCAKES

야채전
YACHE JEON

These are one of my kids' favourite things to eat. In fact, whenever I cook up a batch, they get very excited and exclaim 'Korean Feast!' as they see it as a sign that a big spread of Korean food is imminent. I can't resist *pajeon* (spring onion/scallion pancakes) or *buchu jeon* (garlic chive pancakes), but these days I make this version far more often as they are a great way of getting my boys to eat more vegetables, and they could both easily eat a mountain of these. They're a real crowd pleaser and a good way of using up any vegetables that might be languishing in the fridge.

150 g/5½ oz. plain/all-purpose flour
4 tbsp cornflour/cornstarch
2 tsp baking powder
¼ tsp salt
½ courgette/zucchini
½ carrot
⅛ cabbage (about 150 g/5½ oz.), finely sliced
½ tsp crushed/minced garlic
vegetable oil, for frying

DIPPING SAUCE
8 tbsp Korean soy sauce
4 tbsp Korean apple/rice vinegar

MAKES 9 MINI PANCAKES

Mix the soy sauce and vinegar together for the dipping sauce in a small bowl and set to one side.

In a large bowl, mix the flour, cornflour, baking powder and salt together. Whisk in 125 ml/½ cup water. Grate in the courgette and carrot, add the cabbage and garlic and mix.

Place a large frying pan/skillet over a high heat with 2 tablespoons vegetable oil. Use a tablespoon to drop spoonfuls of the mixture into the pan, making sure they have enough space to spread. This will need to be done in batches so that the pan is not too crowded.

Use the back of the spoon to smooth out each spoonful to make the pancakes about 5-mm/¼-inch thick. Fry for 90 seconds until the bottom of each pancake is golden.

Flip each pancake and add an additional tablespoon of oil into the pan. Fry for 1 minute on the second side. Repeat with the remaining pancake mixture until it has all been used.

Serve with the dipping sauce on the side.

SAUSAGE & RICE CAKE SKEWERS

쏘떡쏘떡

SSOTTEOK SSOTTEOK

The name *ssotteok ssotteok* comes from the combination of *sso* from 'sausage' and *tteok*, which are Korean rice cakes – and on these skewers, the sausage and rice cakes are alternately stacked to become *ssotteok ssotteok*. They are one of my kids' favourite Korean street foods, although sometimes I wonder if it's because they love the fun name more than the food itself! Either way, these are easy to make and bring my kids a lot of joy!

225 g/8 oz. *garae tteok*
   (Korean cylindrical rice cakes)
6 frankfurter sausages
1 tbsp vegetable oil

SAUCE
2 tbsp *gochujang*
   (Korean red pepper paste)
4 tbsp tomato ketchup
4 tbsp honey
½ tsp crushed/minced garlic

10 skewers (if using wooden skewers, soak them for 30 minutes in warm water first)

MAKES 5 SKEWERS

Bring a saucepan of water to the boil. Add the rice cakes and boil for 2 minutes to soften. Drain, rinse under cold water and set to one side.

Place a saucepan over a medium heat and add all the sauce ingredients, along with 3 tablespoons water. Stir and simmer for 2 minutes until the sauce begins to bubble at the sides.

Cut the sausages to the same length as the rice cakes. Skewer the hot dogs and rice cakes in an alternating pattern using 2 skewers each to secure them. Brush both sides of the skewers with vegetable oil.

Place a large frying pan/skillet over a medium-high heat. Fry the skewers for 3 minutes on each side, or until the rice cakes become slightly crisp. Brush with the sauce and serve immediately.

TIP *Skewered street foods are very popular in Korea as they're portable and delicious – so they also make great party food. Serve these alongside the Soy Glazed Chicken Skewers (see page 49) as part of a party buffet spread or as a starter.*

KIMCHI GRILLED CHEESE

There's something magical about the combination of kimchi and cheese. The tangy, spiciness of kimchi complements creamy cheese so perfectly that it's now become a famous marriage of flavours. In Korea, it is common to see these two ingredients paired in all sorts of dishes – from *ramyun* noodles, burger toppings, tacos and fries – kimchi and cheese can be used together in so many ways. So it's not surprising that there are lots of recipes for kimchi grilled cheese sandwiches out there, but I had to include one as it really is the best kind of sandwich – and here, the secret ingredient is the sour cream, which helps glue the mozzarella to the sandwich and also gives it a layer of flavour making these completely irresistible.

110 g/4 oz. kimchi, plus extra
    to serve
1 tbsp vegetable oil
½ tsp *gochujang*
    (Korean red pepper paste)
40 g/3 tbsp spreadable butter
2 slices sourdough bread
2 tbsp sour cream
100 g/3½ oz. mozzarella

SERVES 1

Reserve 2 teaspoons of the kimchi, chop it and set to one side.

Place a frying pan/skillet over a high heat with the oil. Add the remaining kimchi and the *gochujang*, fry for 2 minutes and set to one side.

Butter the bread on both sides of each slice. Spread sour cream on one side of each slice of bread. Layer half the mozzarella over the sour cream on one slice, followed by the cooked kimchi, the reserved chopped kimchi and then the rest of the mozzarella on top. Place the second slice of bread, sour cream-side down, on top.

Place a large frying pan over a medium head and carefully place the sandwich in the middle.

Lay something heavy on top (e.g. a plate with a mortar and pestle on top) or press heavily with a spatula for 2 minutes. Flip and fry for a further 2 minutes until crisp and cooked.

Slice in half and serve immediately with extra kimchi.

SPAM RICE BALLS

주먹밥

JUMEOKBAP

Jumeokbap translates as 'fist rice', as the shape of the rice ball looks similar to the closed fist you make with your hand as the rice is squeezed into shape. It is the perfect alternative to a sandwich, great for picnics and snacks as it is portable, satisfying and you can customize it to have any filling you like. Traditionally, minced beef or tuna mayonnaise are often used, but I've used Spam in this recipe. Don't be shy of Spam! It's admittedly not great to look at as it slides out of the can, but soaking it first is key to getting rid of any excess salt (and fat), then it crisps up to deliciously bacon-y bits in the pan that work so well in this rice!

200 g/7 oz. Spam
1 tbsp vegetable oil
½ carrot, finely diced
1 green jalapeño chilli/chile, finely chopped
2 medium eggs
250 g/2 cups cooked warm sushi rice

SAUCE
1 tbsp Korean soy sauce
1 tsp light soft brown sugar

MAKES 12 BALLS

Place the Spam in a large bowl and cover with boiling water. Leave to soak for 5 minutes.

Meanwhile, mix the sauce ingredients together with 1 teaspoon water in a small bowl.

Remove the Spam from the bowl and pat dry with paper towels. Place on a chopping board and finely dice.

Place a large frying pan/skillet over a high heat with the vegetable oil. Add the Spam and carrot and fry for 5 minutes until the meat is lightly browned and crispy.

Add the chilli, fry for 1 minute, then add the sauce and stir for 30 seconds, or until it is absorbed by the Spam. Tip the mixture into a large mixing bowl and set to one side.

Place the pan back over a high heat and crack the eggs in. Scramble the eggs for 40 seconds, or until just cooked, then tip into the mixing bowl with the Spam mixture. Add the rice to the bowl and mix all the ingredients together.

Take a small handful of rice and squeeze it in the palm of your hands to create a small ball. Repeat with the remaining rice until there are 12 equally sized balls.

Enjoy on its own, dipped in ketchup or eaten with kimchi!

MEAT
& FISH
고기, 생선

WHEN PEOPLE THINK ABOUT KOREAN FOOD, THEY OFTEN THINK OF KOREAN BBQ. Meat (either marinated or plain) is cooked in the middle of the table and served with lettuce leaves to wrap the meat into a *ssam* alongside some pickles and/or kimchi for acidity and a variety of *banchan* (side dishes). It's great sharing food as everyone helps themselves to the meat from the grill to create their own perfect mouthful.

Ssam (lettuce wraps) are not just reserved for meat. Being a peninsula, Korea has some amazing fish and seafood dishes. *Hwe* (raw fish) is popular eaten in lettuce wraps too, and is quite different to the sushi you might be more familiar with as the fish is dispatched and cut to eat immediately, so the flesh is firm rather than soft. It's usually enjoyed with a *gochujang* (Korean red pepper paste) and vinegar-based *chojang* sauce, which gives the *hwe* a spicy, tangy kick.

Despite being born in Busan, I've never been a huge fan of raw fish, which is surprising as my family all love it and my great grandmothers were *hoenyeo* divers. *Hoenyeo* are women divers who free dive into the ocean to catch all sorts of edible treasures, including sea cucumbers, *meongae* (sea pineapple) and even the occasional octopus. These are often sold to be enjoyed as *hwe* (sometimes paired with a glass of *soju* Korean spirit), and I wish that I loved raw fish as I'm always so fascinated watching them dive and would really like to enjoy their catch.

I do, however, love fish when it's cooked. In Korea, we usually serve fish whole with the bones intact. Everyone separates the flesh from the bones at the table as they eat, so the fish stays moist and has the best flavour. I grew up being able to separate the bones from the fish very young and to this day, it's something that my uncle always talks about as he used to be fascinated watching this tiny toddler navigate the small, sharp bones and enjoy eating fish with such relish.

Mackerel is one of my particular favourites and we used to eat it a lot when I was little. We would often eat it grilled, or my mum would braise it in soy sauce and *gochugaru* (Korean red pepper flakes) or with kimchi, and you'll find a recipe for it in this chapter. The meaty, fatty mackerel is the perfect match to tart, spicy kimchi and it's such a speedy meal to throw together.

This section of the book actually has some of my favourite recipes in it – a few of them from my childhood or influenced by my family, and others are ones with a bit of a twist – like the dumpling tacos, which take all the flavours of traditional Korean *mandu* dumplings but make for an easy midweek meal as there's no fiddly folding involved. I hope you love these dishes as much as I do!

PORK BELLY WITH PINEAPPLE & SSAMJANG SAUCE

삼겹살
SAMGYEOPSAL

During the summer of 2024, we all went out to Korea to visit family and do some exploring. One of the big highlights of this trip was a weekend away with my cousins. My cousin, Ji-Hyun, had found a house big enough to fit our four families and there was a great outside space with a barbecue and long picnic tables. My cousins took charge of the food and had brought several kilos of different meats with them including LA galbi beef short ribs, steaks and sausages... but the best bit of the whole meal was the *samgyeopsal* (pork belly) that my cousin, Dong-Gu, grilled on the barbecue with slices of pineapple. Pork belly and pineapple might seem like an obvious combination to many, but it's the first time I'd eaten them with Korean food, and I was really surprised at how well the flavours of the sweet pineapple complemented the earthy, salty *ssamjang* sauce and pork belly.

500 g/1 lb. 2 oz. pork belly,
    cut into 2-cm/¾-inch thick
    slices, rind removed
1 tsp garlic granules
1 tsp salt
vegetable oil, for frying
1 pineapple, peeled, cored and
    cut into 2-cm/¾-inch cubes

SSAMJANG SAUCE
2 tbsp *doenjang*
    (Korean soy bean paste)
1½ tbsp toasted sesame oil
1 tbsp toasted sesame seeds
2 tsp *gochujang*
    (Korean red pepper paste)
1 spring onion/scallion,
    finely chopped
¼ tsp crushed/minced garlic

TO SERVE
lettuce leaves
freshly steamed rice
long red chilli/chile, finely sliced

SERVES 2

Season both sides of each slice of pork belly with the garlic granules and salt. Lay the pork belly on a baking sheet and place in an air fryer at 180°C/350°F for 15 minutes.

After 15 minutes, flip the pork belly slices and place the baking sheet back in the air fryer for a further 10 minutes.

Meanwhile, mix together all the *ssamjang* sauce ingredients with 1 tablespoon water in a small bowl and set to one side.

Place a large frying pan/skillet over a high heat and lightly grease with some vegetable oil. Fry the pineapple for 2 minutes on both sides until golden all over (or leave the pineapple as it is if preferred).

To serve, cut the pineapple and pork belly into bite-sized pieces. Take a lettuce leaf in the palm of your hand and top with rice, pork belly, pineapple, a small smear of *ssamjang* and some sliced chilli. Wrap and put the whole delicious parcel in your mouth!

TIPS *Definitely give this recipe a try for it's delicious salty/sweet taste, but it's even better if you cook it on a barbecue on a summer's day.*

If you want to cook the pork belly in a conventional oven, rather than an air fryer, preheat the oven to 180°C/160°C fan/350°F/Gas 4 and cook for 20 minutes on each side.

KOREAN 'BUFFALO' WINGS

매운 닭날개

MAEUN DAK NALGAE

In Korea, we often eat *chojang* – a spicy, tangy sauce made from *gochujang* (Korean red pepper paste) and vinegar – with raw fish. It's not usually eaten with meat, but the idea of combining those spicy, sharp *chojang* flavours with lots of butter to create a 'buffalo-style' sauce got stuck in my head and the result are these finger-lickingly addictive wings.

I first started cooking wings in this flour mix thanks to Lizzie Mabbott (@hollowlegs on Instagram) and now they are my go-to way of cooking wings. Tossing them in this seasoned mix makes them deliciously crispy and helps any sauce to really cling onto the skin.

4 tbsp plain/all-purpose flour
1 tbsp garlic granules
1 tbsp baking powder
1 tsp salt
½ tsp ground white pepper
1 kg/2¼ lb. chicken wings
spring onions/scallions, chopped,
   to garnish

'BUFFALO' SAUCE
40 g/3 tbsp salted butter
2 tbsp *gochujang*
   (Korean red pepper paste)
1 tbsp *gochugaru*
   (Korean red pepper flakes)
1 tsp caster/granulated sugar
5 tbsp rice vinegar

SERVES 2–4

Line a baking sheet with baking paper.

Mix the flour, garlic granules, baking powder, salt and pepper in a large bowl. Place the chicken wings in the bowl and toss to coat them in the flour mixture. Shake off any excess flour and place them on the lined baking sheet. Put the baking sheet in an air fryer at 180°C/350°F for 20 minutes.

Meanwhile, melt the butter in a saucepan over a medium heat. Add the *gochujang*, *gochugaru*, sugar and 4 tablespoons water. Stir for 1 minute until the sauce begins to bubble, then remove from the heat and stir in the vinegar.

Remove the baking sheet from the air fryer, flip each wing over and cook for another 20 minutes.

Pour the sauce into a large bowl. Add the hot chicken wings and toss them in the sauce until they are well coated.

Serve immediately garnished with spring onions (with plenty of napkins)!

TIP *These can also be baked in the oven if preferred. Preheat the oven to 180°C/160°C fan/350°F/Gas 4, spray a baking sheet with oil to grease, top with the chicken wings and bake for 50 minutes, flipping them over halfway through the cooking time.*

ONE-PAN
CHILLI CHICKEN

DAK GALBI

This spicy chicken is usually served as a sharing dish, cooked in the middle of the table. It is in a *gochujang* (Korean red pepper paste) sauce, but has a hint of curry powder, which gives it a really distinctive flavour. It's a great one to share with friends, is super easy and, at the end, you can fry rice in any remaining sauce with a glug of sesame oil for a really delicious fried rice finish to the meal.

150 g/5½ oz. *garae tteok* (Korean long rice cakes)

600 g/1 lb. 5 oz. boneless chicken thighs (skin on), cut into 2.5-cm/1-inch wide strips

¼ Chinese cabbage (about 250 g/9 oz.), cut into bite-sized pieces

1 sweet potato, peeled and sliced into strips the same size as the rice cakes

½ onion, roughly chopped

2 spring onions/scallions, roughly chopped

pinch of toasted sesame seeds, to garnish

SAUCE

4 tbsp *gochujang* (Korean red pepper paste)

2 tbsp *gochugaru* (Korean red pepper flakes)

2 tbsp Korean soy sauce

2 tbsp mirin

2 tbsp honey

1 tbsp toasted sesame oil

1½ tsp medium curry powder

2 tsp crushed/minced garlic

2-cm/¾-inch piece of fresh ginger, peeled and finely chopped

SERVES 4

Place the rice cakes in a bowl with enough cold water to cover. Leave the to soak for 10 minutes to soften slightly.

Mix all the sauce ingredients with 4 tablespoons water in a small bowl.

Place a large pan over a medium-high heat with the chicken and the sauce. Drain the rice cakes and add to the pan, along with the cabbage, sweet potato and onion, mixing so that everything is coated in the sauce.

Cook for 10–15 minutes until the chicken is cooked through and the sweet potato has softened, stirring occasionally to make sure nothing sticks to the bottom of the pan. If the rice cakes or sweet potato begin to stick, add 2 tablespoons water to loosen them slightly.

Add the spring onions just before serving and garnish with sesame seeds.

KOREAN SMASHED TACOS

Tacos are a huge hit in our house, to the point that for a long time we had 'Taco Tuesdays' each week as our kids are such big fans. Writing this now, I'm not sure why that sort of faded out, I think I need to start it again!

There's been a trend on social media for smashed tacos for a while. This led me to wonder how to make ones with Korean flavours. At around the same time, I was also thinking of ways to make *mandu* (Korean dumplings) easier and faster – and then with a lightbulb moment, these tacos were born. They taste a lot like *mandu* (Korean dumplings), but without the need for any intricate folding, and are a really fun twist on both *mandu* and tacos.

300 g/10½ oz. minced/
 ground pork
2 spring onions/scallions,
 finely chopped
1 tbsp light soy sauce
1 tbsp toasted sesame oil
½ tsp ground white pepper
1 tsp crushed/minced ginger
1 tsp crushed/minced garlic
6 small soft corn tacos

TOPPINGS
kimchi, finely chopped
spring onion/scallion,
 finely chopped
long red chilli/chile,
 finely sliced
sour cream

MAKES 6 TACOS

In a large bowl, mix together the pork, spring onions, soy sauce, sesame oil, white pepper, ginger and garlic. Shape the mixture into 6 equal-sized balls and flatten each ball evenly in the centre of each taco.

Place a large frying pan/skillet over a high heat. Flatten the taco, meat-side down, into the hot pan. Cook for 3–4 minutes until the meat is cooked through.

Serve each taco topped with kimchi, spring onion, chilli and a few dollops of sour cream.

PORK BELLY WITH PADRONS

돼지고기 꽈리고추 볶음
DWEJI GOGI GWALLI GOCHU BOKKEUM

A few years ago, my cousin, Dong-gu, invited us over for dinner at his house during one of our trips to Korea. He's a real foodie and always knows the best places to eat, but this was the first time he'd ever cooked for me. Turns out, he takes his cooking seriously too and he made an amazing spread of grilled fish, loads of *banchan* (side dishes) and *jjigae* (stews), but the one thing that really stood out, was this amazing pork dish with shisito peppers. Shisitos can be pretty tricky to get hold of, but padron peppers make a good substitute, but if you can't find any, you could use a bell pepper cut into bite-sized pieces instead.

½ onion
1 tbsp vegetable oil
125 g/4½ oz. padron peppers, stems removed
500 g/1 lb. 2 oz. pork belly, rind removed and cut into bite-sized pieces
2 tsp crushed/minced garlic
15 g/½ oz. piece of fresh ginger, finely sliced
½ long red chilli/chile, finely sliced (optional)
freshly steamed rice and kimchi, to serve

SAUCE
2 tbsp Korean soy sauce
1 tbsp oyster sauce
1 tbsp light soft brown sugar

SERVES 2

Mix the sauce ingredients with 6 tablespoons water in a small bowl and set to one side.

Grate the onion (or use a food processor) into a paste and set aside.

Place a large frying pan/skillet over a high heat with the vegetable oil. Add the padrons and fry for 2 minutes until they start to blister. Remove from the pan and set to one side.

Add the pork to the pan and fry for 3 minutes, turning so that the pork browns all over. Remove from the pan and set to one side.

Add the onion, garlic and ginger to the pan and fry for 2 minutes. Pour in the sauce, fry for 2 minutes and then stir in the pork and padrons. Finish with the sliced chilli on top.

Serve with freshly steamed rice and kimchi.

KOREAN SOY MARINATED STEAK

Bulgogi is usually beef cut into wafer-thin slices and marinated in a sweet soy sauce. This can be a sharing dish in the middle of a table, as a topping for *bibimbap* (mixed rice), as a filling for *kimbap* (seaweed rolls) or simply served over rice. It's super quick to make and one of the go-to recipes for many Korean households.

In Korea, it's easy to get the ready-sliced *bulgogi* beef in any supermarket but unless you have easy access to a Korean store, this is trickier elsewhere. You could freeze steaks to firm them up before slicing if making *bulgogi* at home, but unless you're very confident with a knife, it is hard to get the slices really, really thin, so there's the risk of ending up with chewy strips (and a waste) of beef.

This is my super-quick alternative – the sweet, salty, soy flavours of the *bulgogi* sauce, but dressed over a steak that can be cooked to your preference so that the meat is succulent and tender. Serve simply over rice, in *ssam* (lettuce wraps) or with a salad as a great midweek meal.

2 sirloin steaks
    (weighing about 225 g/8 oz. each)
1 tbsp vegetable oil
salt
lettuce leaves, for wrapping
your choice of *banchan*, to serve

SWEET SOY SAUCE
3 garlic cloves
1 apple, peeled, cored and cut
    into chunks
3 spring onions/scallions,
    roughly chopped
6 tbsp Korean soy sauce
1 tbsp toasted sesame oil
2 tbsp light soft brown sugar
¼ tsp ground white pepper

**SERVES 4 (WITH BANCHAN SIDES)
OR 2 WITHOUT SIDES**

Put all the sauce ingredients into a food processor with 150 ml/⅔ cup water and blitz together. Pour the sauce into a small saucepan over a medium-high heat and simmer for 5 minutes.

Coat the steaks with the oil and season with salt on each side.

Place a large frying pan/skillet over a high heat. Fry the steaks for about 3 minutes on each side (or until the steak is cooked to your liking).

Spoon the sauce over the steaks, making sure they're completely coated and cook over a high heat for 1 minute.

Remove the steaks from the pan and rest on a chopping board for 5 minutes. Slice and serve with steamed rice, lettuce leaves and your choice of *banchan* (side dishes).

GOCHUJANG & HONEY GLAZED CHICKEN THIGHS

고추장 닭다리
GOCHUJANG DAK DARI

These sticky, glossy chicken thighs are sweet and spicy and are a welcome addition to any salad, bowl of rice or even between a couple of slices of good bread for a truly epic sandwich. The key to making this chicken really great is to use deboned chicken thighs with the skin on. That way, you get the full flavour of the skin, succulent meat and a quick cooking time. Deboning the thighs is worth the extra effort – ask a friendly butcher to do this for you to make things even quicker!

3 tbsp honey
2 tbsp *gochujang*
    (Korean red pepper paste)
1 tbsp toasted sesame oil
2 tsp crushed/minced garlic
½ tsp crushed/minced ginger
1 kg/2¼ lb. chicken thighs,
    skin on and deboned
chopped spring onions/scallions,
    to serve

SERVES 4

Preheat the oven to 200°C/180°C fan/400°F/Gas 6.

Mix the honey, *gochujang*, sesame oil, garlic and ginger together in a bowl and set to one side.

If the chicken thighs still have bones, carefully cut the bones away. Place the deboned chicken into a bowl with half of the marinade and mix, making sure they are thoroughly coated.

Line a baking sheet with baking paper (for easier washing up). Lay the chicken on the baking sheet, skin-side up, and place in the oven for 20 minutes.

Remove from the oven, brush with the remaining sauce and return to the oven for a further 10 minutes to become sticky and glossy.

Serve with the marinade from the baking sheet spooned on top and sprinkled with spring onions.

TIP *If you feel intimidated by the prospect of deboning the chicken thighs, don't worry, this sauce will work just as well with bone-in thighs too; just add an extra 15 minutes to the cooking time.*

SWEET & SOUR PRAWNS

탕수새우
TANG SU SAE WOO

When you go to a Chinese restaurant in Korea, there's usually a handful of go-to dishes that everyone orders: *jjambbong* (spicy seafood noodle soup), *jjajjangmyun* (black bean noodles) and *tangsuyeok* (sweet and sour pork). *Jjambbong* is one of my absolute favourites but *tangsuyeok* is also pretty irresistible. This prawn version is a quicker, lighter, sweet and sour dish, which is equally delicious (possibly even more so) than the more commonly ordered pork dish and can be on the table in less than 20 minutes.

250 g/9 oz. raw king prawns/jumbo shrimp, shelled and deveined
3 tbsp cornflour/cornstarch
3 tbsp vegetable oil
1 red (bell) pepper, chopped
½ onion, chopped
2 garlic cloves, finely sliced
½ long red chilli/chile, finely sliced
2 tbsp rice wine vinegar
freshly steamed rice, to serve

SAUCE
4 tbsp Korean soy sauce
5 tbsp tomato ketchup
¼ tsp ground white pepper
3½ tbsp caster/superfine sugar

SERVES 2

Mix the sauce ingredients together in a small bowl and set to one side.

Place the prawns in a bowl, add 2 tablespoons water and mix (this will make them sticky enough to coat in the cornflour). Drain any excess water, add the cornflour and toss so that the prawns are lightly coated.

Place a large frying pan/skillet over a high heat with the vegetable oil. Fry the prawns for 1 minute on each side, making sure to give them enough space so that they don't stick together. Remove the prawns from the pan and set to one side.

Place the pan back over a high heat and add the red pepper, onion, garlic and chilli and fry for 2 minutes. Add the sauce and simmer for 1 minute, making sure to coat all the vegetables in the sauce.

Return the prawns to the pan and stir to coat in the sauce. Mix in the vinegar and serve with freshly steamed rice.

TUNA & CHILLI LETTUCE WRAPS

I'll often have variations of this for lunch as it's really quick, healthy, and I usually have all the ingredients handy as it mainly uses store-cupboard items. Canned tuna is really popular in Korea and you can buy it in lots of different sauces, from *jjajjang* (black bean) to kimchi flavour. I love the ones in a spicy sauce, like this recipe, which is deliciously refreshing when wrapped in the lettuce leaves.

100 g/3½ oz. tuna in spring water, drained
1 baby gem lettuce, leaves separated
1 portion of freshly steamed rice

SAUCE
1½ tsp *gochujang*
    (Korean red pepper paste)
½ long red chilli/chile, sliced
2½ tsp toasted sesame oil
1 tsp toasted sesame seeds
½ spring onion/scallion,
    finely chopped

SERVES 1

Mix the sauce ingredients in a medium bowl. Add the tuna and mix into the sauce.

To eat, take a lettuce leaf in the palm of your hand, top with rice and a spoonful of the spicy tuna mixture. Wrap and try to fit it all into your mouth in one mouthful!

TIP *To add extra flavour, top with Quick Cut Kimchi (see page 16) or Soy Pickled Onions (see page 24).*

KOREAN CHILLI MUSSELS

My mum and dad used to own a caravan down in Devon. We would stay there at every opportunity as we loved the beautiful beaches and fantastic produce the area has to offer. One of the highlights of our trips was visiting the local fishmonger, where we would always buy a selection of fish, shellfish and crab to cook a seafood feast in the evenings after spending the day building fortresses and castles with our boys on the sandy beaches. My mum kept a 'basic' supply of Korean ingredients in the cupboard handy, so this mussel dish was thrown together one evening using these store-cupboard essentials with the help of some fresh garlic, ginger and chilli to create the most delicious sauce. Make sure you eat this with something to soak it all up (either rice or chunky crusty bread). It's the perfect dish for a summer's evening, and takes only minutes to put together.

500 g/1 lb. 2 oz. mussels, cleaned and debearded
1½ tbsp vegetable oil
1 onion, finely diced
1 long red chilli/chile, finely chopped
3 spring onions/scallions, finely chopped
freshly steamed rice or crusty bread, to serve

SAUCE
2 tbsp *gochugaru* (Korean red pepper flakes)
2 tbsp Korean soy sauce
1 tbsp toasted sesame oil
1 tbsp mirin
2 tsp light soft brown sugar
1 tsp crushed/minced ginger
1 tsp crushed/minced garlic
¼ tsp ground white pepper

SERVES 2

Tap any open mussels and discard any that do not close.

Mix the sauce ingredients together in a small bowl.

Place a frying pan/skillet over a medium heat with the vegetable oil. Add the onion and fry for about 3–4 minutes until translucent and soft. Add the sauce to the pan and fry for 1 minute.

Turn the heat up to high and then add the mussels. Stir to coat them in the sauce and keep stirring for 5 minutes until the mussels have opened. Discard any that remain closed.

Add the chilli and spring onions. Give everything a final stir and serve immediately with rice or chunky slices of bread to mop up all the sauce.

BRAISED MACKEREL WITH KIMCHI

고등어 김치 조림
GODEUNGA KIMCHI JORIM

Growing up, we always had cans of pilchards or mackerel in the cupboard. They are such a handy, nutritious store-cupboard ingredient and my mum would usually cook it braised in soy sauce and *gochugaru* (Korean chilli flakes) or this way, with ripe, tangy kimchi. The mackerel is soft and spicy, and you can eat it simply with some rice, or in a lettuce wrap for a quick *ssam* meal that you can get on the table in around 15 minutes.

1 tbsp vegetable oil
200 g/7 oz. kimchi
1 x 400-g/14-oz. can of mackerel
   or pilchards in spring water,
   drained
1 tbsp *gochugaru*
   (Korean chilli flakes)
freshly steamed rice and thinly
   sliced spring onion/scallion,
   to serve

SERVES 2

Heat the vegetable oil in a saucepan over a high heat and fry the kimchi for 3–4 minutes.

Add the mackerel and *gochugaru* and use a pair of tongs to make sure the fish is coated in the kimchi and *gochugaru*. Fry for 5 minutes, then add 250 ml/1 cup water, bring to the boil and cook for a further 5 minutes.

Serve with steamed rice and thinly sliced spring onions.

TIPS *Make sure to use properly fermented kimchi (it should be tangy and sour) for the best flavour.*

Whole chunks of mackerel/pilchards work best in this recipe as the fillets easily break apart. Sometimes, I've only been able to get hold of tinned mackerel in tomato sauce rather than spring water, which works fine but makes for a sweeter dish. To maintain the flavour of the kimchi, give the tinned fish a quick rinse first.

SOUPS
& STEWS
국, 찌개, 탕

I ALWAYS THINK OF SOUPS AND STEWS TO BE THE REAL COMFORT FOOD OF KOREA. When I was recovering from my time in hospital, I was so thankful to have my mum's soups stocked up in the fridge (with extra portions in the freezer). Soups are always served very hot, often in an earthenware bowl to retain the heat, as the temperature of food is really important to Koreans. Funnily enough, when Koreans eat their piping hot soup, they often exclaim, 'ah, siwonhada!', which translates as 'so refreshing!', but really that refers to how invigorated, rejuvenated and cleansed they feel from the inside out after eating a hot soup.

Soups are eaten with most meals in Korea and come in various forms: *guk* are quick, light soups that are usually served in individual bowls; *tang* are chunkier soups that take a little longer to simmer; and *jjigae* are heartier, thicker stews that can be eaten as individual portions, but are also often served in the middle of the table to share. At barbecue restaurants in Korea, an earthenware bowl of *doenjang jjigae* (soybean paste stew) is often placed directly on the barbecue to be enjoyed bubbling hot. These *jjigae* often contain meat offcuts, which give them extra flavour, and are one of my favourite parts of the meal.

Korean soups and stews are usually made from a dried anchovy stock, which rather than tasting fishy, give the broths depth. However, now that I don't live in London, I've discovered how tricky these can be to get hold of, so I often use chicken stock as a replacement. Fresh chicken stock gives the best flavour, but if you're using instant stock cubes, just make sure not to use ones that have any additional herbs as they can really change the overall taste of the soup, and opt for the 'low salt' versions as the recipes here already feature seasonings of soy sauce or fish sauce.

For those soups that I feel really do need the anchovy stock base, I've suggested using *dashi* powder instead, which is a little easier to get hold of than dried anchovies and can often be found in the Japanese section of an Asian supermarket. If you do live near a Korean supermarket, then you can replace any of the stocks in this section with the anchovy stock recipe on page 90 for a more authentic Korean flavour. Dried anchovies come in various sizes but it's the large ones that you'll need for making stocks – they create a mild, clean stock with a savoury umami.

SPINACH & SOY BEAN SOUP

This has got to be one of the easiest, quickest soups there is. It's ready in under 10 minutes and is delicious served simply with a bowl of steamed rice or as part of a larger Korean meal. Traditionally, the Korean table is filled with a large selection of different *banchan* (side dishes) and kimchi to share in the middle, then each person gets their own individual bowl of rice and *guk* (soup). *Doenjang guk* is one of the most popular, with a few different variations. I've added tofu here, but you could leave it out and/or add mushrooms too.

800 ml/3⅓ cups water
   (or anchovy stock, see below)
1 tsp dashi powder
1 tbsp *doenjang*
   (Korean soy bean paste)
175 g/6 oz. firm tofu, drained and
   cut into 2-cm/1-inch squares
1 garlic clove, sliced
¼ medium heat, any colour chilli/
   chile, sliced (optional)
50 g/1 cup baby spinach
2 spring onions/scallions, finely
   chopped
freshly steamed rice, to serve

SERVES 2

Place a saucepan over a high heat with the water and dashi powder. If using the anchovy stock, leave the dashi powder out.

Bring to the boil, then add the *doenjang*. Use a spoon to press any lumps against the inside of the pan so that it dissolves into the water. Add the tofu, garlic, chilli and spinach.

Boil for 3 minutes, top with spring onions, then serve with steamed rice.

ANCHOVY STOCK

MYEULCHI YOOKSU

10–15 large dried anchovies
   (around a handful), roughly
   5 cm/2 inches long
5 pieces of *dashima* (dried kelp),
   roughly 5-cm/2-inch squares
350 g/12 oz. mooli, roughly
   chopped
½ onion, roughly chopped
3 spring onions/scallions,
   roughly chopped

MAKES ABOUT 1.8 LITRES/QUARTS

Add all the ingredients to a large saucepan with 2 litres/quarts water. Bring to the boil for 15 minutes and skim off any foam from the surface, then leave to cool.

Once the stock has completely cooled, it can be frozen for up to 3 months.

TIP *To make a vegetable stock, replace the anchovies with 4–5 dried shiitake mushrooms.*

3-INGREDIENT KIMCHI STEW

김치 찌개
KIMCHI JJIGAE

Kimchi jjigae is one of my favourite Korean dishes. It's spicy, comforting and is the very first dish that I remember my mum teaching me how to make when I was younger. It's so full of flavour that you don't even need lots of *banchan* (side dishes) with it. This is a really simple recipe, using just a few ingredients – ones that you might possibly have to hand. Traditionally, firm tofu would be used (or specifically, a medium-firm tofu made especially for *jjigae* stews), but I love the texture of silken tofu and it is easy to find in the ambient aisle of most supermarkets so you can keep it handy in your cupboard for when your *kimchi jjigae* craving hits.

1 tbsp vegetable oil
350 g/12½ oz. kimchi,
    roughly chopped
100 g/3½ oz. tuna in water,
    drained
350 g/12½ oz. silken tofu,
    cut into bite-sized pieces

TO SERVE
chopped spring onions/scallions
freshly steamed rice
gochugaru (Korean red pepper
    flakes)

SERVES 2

Heat the vegetable oil in a saucepan over a medium heat. Using a pair of tongs, add the kimchi to the pan (reserving any kimchi liquid) and fry for 3–4 minutes until glossy.

Pour in 500 ml/2 cups water and any reserved kimchi juice. Turn up the heat to high, bring to the boil and cook for 5 minutes.

Add the tuna and warm through for 2 minutes. Add the tofu and simmer for an a further 2 minutes.

Serve bubbling hot, garnished with spring onions, with freshly steamed rice and some *gochugaru* to taste.

TIPS *To make a great kimchi jjigae, always use ripe, sour kimchi and secondly make sure to spend the time to fry the kimchi to ensure maximum flavour (even when using minimal ingredients).*

If you're not a tuna fan, you could use Spam or thinly sliced pork belly instead.

SIMPLE COD SOUP

This is a lovely soup with a clear, clean broth. We usually describe this kind of soup as *siwonhada*, which translates as 'cooling'. 'Refreshing' is probably more accurate as it refers to how your body feels, like it is being cleansed and invigorated after eating it. It's usually made with cod steaks, but I've used fillets here for a quicker soup and kelp to create a stock for the extra flavour that you would usually get from the bones of the fish.

150 g/5½ oz. mooli, peeled, cut in half lengthways, then into 5-mm/¼-inch slices
5 g/¼ oz. *dashima* (dried kelp) (or a 5-cm/2-inch square piece)
2 garlic cloves, sliced
1 medium heat chilli/chile, sliced, plus extra to garnish
250 g/9 oz. cod fillets, skin removed and cut into 5-cm/ 2-inch pieces
1 tbsp light soy sauce
2½ tbsp fish sauce
2 spring onions/scallions, finely chopped
freshly steamed rice and kimchi, to serve

SERVES 2

Place the mooli, kelp, garlic and chilli into a pan with 800 ml/3⅓ cups water over a high heat. Bring the water to the boil and skim away any foam from the surface.

After 5 minutes, reduce the heat to medium and remove the kelp. Add the cod, soy sauce, fish sauce and simmer for a further 2–3 minutes, or until the cod is just cooked.

Finish with the spring onions and some extra red chilli, and serve with rice and kimchi.

TIP Daegu *literally translates as 'cod' – but you could replace it with any other firm white fish, such as haddock.*

BEEF & MOOLI SOUP

소고기무국
SOGOGI MUGUK

This is a really quick, simple soup that can be made in 10 minutes. It usually doesn't have any chilli/chile added, so is often one of the first soups for toddlers in Korea, but it's also got enough beefy flavour to satisfy the whole family – although I always like to add a little bit of sliced chilli at the end of mine for some heat. In Korea, when you add rice to a soup, you say '*ma-la*' and I like to *ma-la* my rice in this soup so that you get spoonfuls of rice and soup together in one delicious mouthful.

2 tsp vegetable oil

1 tsp toasted sesame oil

200 g/7 oz. sirloin, any excess fat and sinew removed and steak cut into 5-mm/¼-inch thick strips

pinch of salt

¼ tsp freshly ground black pepper

200 g/7 oz. mooli, peeled and cut into 2cm cubes

1 tsp crushed/minced garlic

1 tbsp light soy sauce

1½ tbsp fish sauce

2 spring onions/scallions, finely chopped

sliced red chilli/chile, to garnish (optional)

freshly steamed rice and kimchi, to serve

SERVES 2

Place a saucepan over a high heat with the vegetable oil and sesame oil. Add the steak with the salt and pepper and fry for 2 minutes. Add the mooli and garlic and fry for a further 2 minutes.

Pour in 800 ml/3⅓ cups water and bring to the boil. Skim off any foam that appears on the surface and cook over a high heat for 5 minutes. Season with the light soy sauce and fish sauce.

Garnish with spring onions and chilli and serve with rice and kimchi.

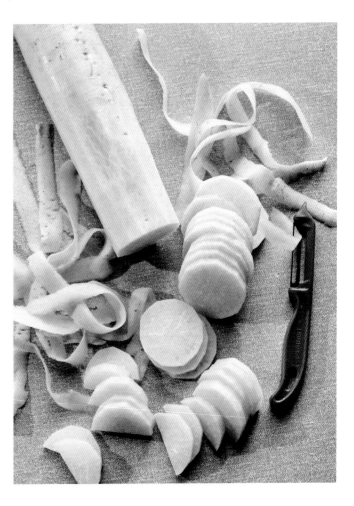

10-MINUTE DUMPLING SOUP

We always have a stash of *mandu* (frozen dumplings) in the freezer. They are handy as a *banchan* (side dish) when we have Korean food, for lunchboxes, and also this super speedy 10-minute soup. *Mandu guk* is traditionally eaten on Lunar New Year's Day with the addition of circular *tteok* rice cakes to bring good luck. These aren't always easy to get hold of, so I've left them out of this recipe, but if you come across them, add at the same time as the *mandu* dumplings to make this hearty soup even more filling.

2 medium eggs
2 spring onions/scallions, finely chopped
2 tbsp light soy sauce
2 tsp crushed/minced garlic
12 frozen *mandu* (Korean dumplings)
¼ tsp ground white pepper

SERVES 2

Whisk the eggs in a small bowl and set to one side.

Fill a saucepan with 750 ml/3 cups water, set over a high heat and bring to the boil. Add the white part of the spring onions to the pan and set the green part to one side.

Add the light soy sauce, garlic, *mandu* and white pepper. Stir to prevent the *mandu* from sticking together. Cook over a high heat for 7–8 minutes until the *mandu* are cooked through.

Pour the egg into the pan in a circular motion and cook for about 30–40 seconds until the egg is just cooked.

Ladle the soup into bowls and finish with the reserved spring onion greens on top.

TIP *I sometimes like to make this soup a little more nutritious by adding a handful of baby spinach or a couple of pak choi for the last minute of cooking time.*

콩나물 김치국
KIMCHI KONGNAMUL GUK

BEANSPROUT & KIMCHI SOUP

Soups containing beansprouts are often considered revitalizing, so combined with chilli/chile heat, this is a popular soup to combat a hangover the morning after a heavy night. It's also a great one to make when you're in a hurry as it only takes a few minutes to throw together.

500 ml/2 cups chicken stock
200 g/7 oz. kimchi, cut into
   bite-sized pieces
½ tsp crushed/minced garlic
125 g/2 cups beansprouts
2 tsp fish sauce
1 spring onion/scallion, finely chopped
½ long red chilli/chile, finely sliced
freshly steamed rice, to serve

SERVES 2

Place a saucepan over a high heat with the chicken stock and kimchi. Bring to the boil and cook for 5 minutes.

Add the garlic, beansprouts and fish sauce. Place a lid on top and leave to cook for a further 5 minutes.

Add the spring onion and chilli and serve bubbling hot with freshly steamed rice.

고추장 찌개
GOCHUJANG JJIGAE

SPICY KOREAN CHILLI STEW

This is a spicy, warming stew, which is easily made with store-cupboard ingredients. We always have *gochujang, gochugaru* and soy sauce to hand at home, so this is a great soup for when we haven't had time to do much of a food shop but need something satisfying in a hurry. You can use any mushrooms here, just roughly tear them to provide texture. The potatoes are the best bit – they soak up all the flavours, so make sure not to miss them out!

1 tbsp vegetable oil
4 spring onions/scallions, finely chopped
1.2 litres/5 cups chicken stock
2 potatoes (about 350 g/12½ oz. in weight),
   unpeeled and cut into bite-sized chunks
2 tbsp *gochujang* (Korean red pepper paste)
1 tbsp *gochugaru* (Korean red pepper flakes)
3 tbsp light soy sauce
1 tsp crushed/minced garlic
½ courgette/zucchini, cut into 1-cm/½-inch thick
   slices
100 g/3½ oz. mushrooms, roughly torn
1 tsp toasted sesame oil
freshly steamed rice, to serve

SERVES 2-3

Place a large saucepan over a medium heat, add the oil and fry the spring onions for 2 minutes. Add the stock and bring to the boil over a high heat.

Add the potatoes, along with the *gochujang, gochugaru*, soy sauce and garlic and boil for 10 minutes. Add the courgette and mushrooms and boil for a further 5 minutes.

Finish with the sesame oil and serve with freshly steamed rice.

MILD SILKEN
TOFU STEW

Soondubu jjigae, in its usual form, is one of my favourite Korean soups and my
go-to order at any Korean restaurant. It's usually a vibrant red and the spicy chilli
is the perfect contrast to the creamy silken tofu. My sons are huge tofu fans, but
the spicy version is too hot for them, so I made them this mild version, which is still
full of flavour but mild enough for everyone to enjoy.

10 g/¼ oz. dried mushrooms
   (such as dried shiitake)
1 litre/4 cups boiling water
2 garlic cloves, sliced
2 spring onions/scallions,
   finely chopped
1 long red chilli/chile (optional)
½ courgette/zucchini, sliced into
   5-mm/1¼-inch half-moons
3 tbsp fish sauce
3 tbsp light soy sauce
450 g/1 lb. silken tofu,
   roughly broken
2 tbsp toasted sesame seeds
2 tbsp toasted sesame oil
freshly steamed rice, to serve

SERVES 2–3

Place the dried mushrooms in a large saucepan and add the boiling water.
Set to one side for 30 minutes for the mushrooms to rehydrate.

Remove the mushrooms using a slotted spoon, leaving the soaking liquid
in the pan. Finely chop the mushrooms and then return them to the pan.

Place the saucepan over a high heat and add the garlic, spring onions, chilli
and courgette. Bring to the boil for 5 minutes. Add the fish sauce, soy
sauce and tofu and cook for a further 5 minutes.

Add the sesame seeds and sesame oil to finish and serve bubbling hot
with freshly steamed rice.

SPICY SEAFOOD STEW

해물탕

HAEMULTANG

Haemultang is a real restaurant dish. It's usually served in a big pan in the middle of the table to finish cooking, and everyone helps themselves to spoonfuls of the delicious seafood. Often, there's a real assortment of shellfish, such as crabs, abalone and clams – all in their shells for maximum flavour – but I wanted to create a version that was easy enough to make for a midweek dinner, so I just use a seafood mix here to keep things simple.

3 tbsp fish sauce
600 g /1 lb. 5 oz. mixed seafood
2 tbsp cornflour/cornstarch
300 g/10½ oz. beansprouts
2 spring onions/scallions,
  roughly chopped
freshly steamed rice, to serve

SAUCE
3 tbsp *gochugaru*
  (Korean red pepper flakes)
3 tbsp mirin
2 tbsp granulated sugar
1 tbsp *gochujang*
  (Korean red pepper paste)
1 tbsp crushed/minced garlic

SERVES 4

In a small bowl, mix together the sauce ingredients.

Place a large, shallow casserole dish (or deep frying pan/skillet) over a high heat. Fill with 1 litre/4 cups water and add the fish sauce. Bring to the boil and once boiling, stir in the sauce and seafood and cook for 3 minutes.

Meanwhile, mix the cornflour with 4 tablespoons water in a small bowl. Stir this into the pan and continue cooking over a high heat for 2 minutes.

Add the beansprouts and spring onions and cook for a final 1 minute until just wilted.

Serve with freshly steamed rice.

RICE & NOODLES
밥, 면

NO MEAL IS COMPLETE WITHOUT RICE OR NOODLES. Most meals (breakfast, lunch and dinner) in Korea are eaten with an individual bowl of rice and would feel lacking without it – unless you're eating noodles. Growing up, I always loved having a Korean breakfast with a bowl of rice, kimchi, an assortment of *banchan* (side dishes) and soup whenever we visited my aunt in Korea. Rice is such an essential food and the smell of it as it steams is so incredibly comforting to most Koreans. A simple bowl of rice can be eaten with a splash of soy sauce and a fried egg for a quick lunch, leftover rice can be fried for a speedy dinner, and rice is also made into *juk* (rice porridge) whenever anyone is feeling poorly to help nurse them back to health.

The only time that rice takes a back seat is when noodles are eaten. Noodles are especially popular at lunchtime because they're quick to make, serve and eat, and are substantial enough to be a meal on their own. My mum is a huge fan of noodles and she can finish a bowlful at quite an astounding speed – noodles are her go-to lunch, and these days I usually have noodles for lunch, too.

In Korea, noodle restaurants often have long lines snaking down the street at lunchtimes, but the queues generally move pretty quickly as everyone is in a hurry to get back to work. Certain areas are famed for particular types of noodles – there's a *kalguksu* (knife-cut noodle soup) alley hidden within the market at Namdaemun in Seoul. Noodles are even a popular picnic food along the banks of the Han River as people buy bowls of instant *ramyun* noodles (plus any extra toppings) at local convenience stores, which all have an instant noodle station where you can help yourself to hot water and use the microwave to prepare them.

As well as *kalguksu* and *ramyun*, there are lots of different types of noodles eaten in Korea, with my favourites being: *somyun* (thin wheat noodles), *dangmyeon* (chewy sweet potato noodles) and *naengmyeon* (buckwheat noodles). *Naengmyeon* noodles are often eaten as a side to Korean BBQ as they provide a lovely contrast to the sweet marinades of the meat. There are also lots of restaurants specializing in big bowls of icy cold noodles, and although the idea of cold noodles might seem unusual, they are a great way to cool down in the hot Korean summer, and they are the best thing to make when you are too hot to eat anything else.

KIMCHI NOODLES

This is the most perfect recipe for hot summer weather. On those summer days when you don't feel like eating much because you're feeling so sticky, the air is hot and you are just craving something fresh – these are the noodles for you. It can be thrown together in less than 10 minutes, there's very little chopping involved (you don't even need to get the chopping board out, a pair of scissors will do), and the tangy, spicy sauce combined with the cool noodles, really wakes up your taste buds and leaves you feeling refreshed.

165 g/6 oz. *somyun*
  (thin wheat noodles)
handful of ice cubes
5-g/¼-oz. pack of salted
  snack seaweed
2 soft-boiled/cooked eggs (optional)
1 spring onion/scallion, finely chopped,
  to garnish

KIMCHI & SOY SAUCE
2 tsp Korean soy sauce
2 tsp *gochujang*
  (Korean red pepper paste)
150 g/5½ oz. kimchi, roughly chopped
1½ tsp toasted sesame oil
1 tbsp toasted sesame seeds
2 spring onions/scallions
  finely chopped

SERVES 2

Place a large saucepan of water over a high heat. Bring to the boil, add the noodles and boil for 3–4 minutes.

Meanwhile, mix all the sauce ingredients in a mixing bowl.

Drain the noodles and rinse under cold water. Mix the noodles into the sauce and add the ice. Crush the seaweed in the packet and scatter on top of the noodles. Top with a runny boiled egg, if using and spring onions.

HAND-TORN DUMPLINGS

수제비
SUJEBI

Sujebi are hand-torn dumplings made from a simple dough and simply dropped into a hot pan of bubbling stock until soft and slightly chewy. Traditionally, they are cooked in an anchovy stock, but this version uses chicken stock and cooked chicken, which add flavour and also make the soup feel even more nourishing. It's a humble soup that doesn't require lots of expensive ingredients – in fact, my mum often talks about how my Korean *halmani* (grandmother) would make this for her growing up, but a very simple version, cooked without any seasonings or additions, and yet she remembers it so fondly as it is such a comfort food. The soup itself is quite neutral in flavour but is served with the *yangnyeom jang* (soy seasoning sauce) in the middle of the table so that everyone can season it to their own liking.

1 courgette/zucchini

2 potatoes

2 litres/quarts chicken stock

2 garlic cloves, peeled and finely sliced

150 g/5½ oz. cooked chicken, cut into bite-sized pieces

4 spring onions/scallions, roughly chopped, plus extra to garnish

2 tbsp fish sauce

2 bird's eye chillies/chiles, finely chopped, to garnish (optional)

DOUGH

350 g/2⅔ cups plain/ all-purpose flour

2 tsp vegetable oil

½ tsp salt

SOY SEASONING SAUCE

8 tbsp Korean soy sauce

1 tbsp fish sauce

1 tbsp *gochugaru* (Korean dried chilli flakes)

3 spring onions/scallions, finely chopped

SERVES 4

First, make the dough. In a large bowl, mix the flour, oil and salt with 130 ml/½ cup water with the back of a spoon until the mixture starts to stick together. Once a rough dough has been formed, use your hands to stick the ball of dough to any powdery bits of flour left in the bowl. Knead for 5 minutes. Place the ball of dough into a food bag and leave for about 30 minutes to rest.

Meanwhile, cut the courgette into half moons, about 5 mm/¼ inch thick. Peel the potatoes and cut to a similar thickness.

In a small bowl, mix together the soy seasoning sauce ingredients and set to one side.

After 30 minutes, knead the dough for another 5 minutes until smooth and elastic.

Place a large saucepan over a high heat with the chicken stock. Once boiling, add the garlic and the potatoes and boil for 3–4 minutes until slightly softened, then add the courgette and cooked chicken.

Flatten and stretch the dough to about 5 mm/¼ inch thick in your hands, then tear off bite-sized pieces and drop into the boiling stock until all the dough is used up. Work quickly to make sure the pieces all cook at a similar time.

Stir to avoid the *sujebi* sticking to each other or the bottom of the pan. Add the spring onions and fish sauce and boil for 3–4 minute,s or until the *sujebi* float to the surface.

Serve immediately, garnished with sliced chilli and spring onions and with the soy seasoning sauce on the side.

간장면
GANJANG MYEON

KID'S SOY SAUCE NOODLES

I'm fairly sure that most children in Korea grow up eating these noodles – I know I certainly did and my children, particularly my youngest, love them too. They are really quick to throw together and are simply flavoured with soy sauce and sesame oil so are great when you need dinner in a hurry, especially when there's hungry mouths to feed.

165 g/6 oz. *somyun*
    (thin wheat noodles)
2 tbsp toasted sesame seeds
1½ tbsp Korean soy sauce
1 tbsp toasted sesame oil
5-g/¼-oz. pack of salted
    snack seaweed (optional)

SERVES 2

Place a large saucepan of water over a high heat and bring to the boil. Add the noodles and cook for about 3 minutes. Drain and rinse under cold running water.

Place the noodles into a mixing bowl and add the sesame seeds, soy sauce and sesame oil, mixing everything together. Squeeze the packet of snack seaweed, if using, to crush it into flakes.

Divide the noodles into 2 bowls and top with the crushed seaweed flakes.

고추기름 마늘면
GOCHU GIREUM MANEUL MYEON

SPEEDY CHILLI OIL NOODLES

Chilli oil noodles are not a traditional Korean dish, but I love chilli oil and wanted to make a version with a Korean twist. The smoky *gochugaru* (Korean red pepper flakes) give these noodles a distinctively Korean flavour. Add your choice of green vegetables – I like to add pak choi/boy choy and/or spinach, which I throw in at the end to wilt.

85 g/3 oz. dried udon or soba noodles
1 spring onion/scallion, finely chopped
½ tsp crushed/minced garlic
½ tsp crushed/minced ginger
1 tbsp Korean soy sauce
1 tbsp *gochugaru* (Korean red pepper flakes)
1½ tbsp oyster sauce
1 tsp toasted sesame oil
3 tbsp vegetable oil
1 tbsp toasted sesame seeds
1 boiled egg (or Soy-marinated Egg, page 22),
    halved, to serve (optional)

SERVES 1

Place a large saucepan of water over a high heat and bring to the boil. Add the noodles and cook according to the packet instructions (usually about 5 minutes). Drain the noodles and rinse under cold water, then set to one side.

Meanwhile, put the spring onion, garlic, ginger, soy sauce, *gochugaru*, oyster sauce and sesame oil in a bowl and mix to make a sauce.

Heat the vegetable oil in a frying pan/skillet until smoking. Pour the hot oil over the sauce ingredients and mix. Add the noodles and mix so that they are well coated. Serve topped with sesame seeds (and the egg, if using).

SWEET POTATO NOODLES WITH BEANSPROUTS

Here's a secret. I much prefer this spicy version to regular *japchae*. You might have heard of *japchae* before – stir-fried sweet potato noodles with assorted vegetables in a sweet, soy sauce. It's often eaten on celebration dates and it's a colourful dish as all the vegetables are fried separately to maintain their vibrant colours. This version is much simpler and the spicy sauce clings onto the noodles, completely transforming the dish. A deliciously quick stir-fry for a midweek dinner.

100 g/3½ oz. *dangmyun*
   (sweet potato noodles)
1 tbsp vegetable oil
200 g/1¾ cups beansprouts
2 spring onions/scallions,
   finely chopped
½ carrot, finely sliced
¼ onion, finely sliced
1 tbsp toasted sesame seeds

SAUCE

1 tbsp *gochujang*
   (Korean red pepper paste)
1 tbsp *gochugaru*
   (Korean red pepper flakes)
2 tbsp caster/granulated sugar
1 tsp crushed/minced garlic
1 tsp toasted sesame oil
1 tsp fish sauce

SERVES 2

Place a large saucepan of water over a high heat. Bring to the boil and add the *dangmyun*, making sure they are completely submerged. Boil the noodles for about 5–6 minutes until softened, then drain, rinse under cold water and set to one side.

Mix the sauce ingredients with 2 tablespoons water in a small bowl.

Place a frying pan/skillet over a high heat with the vegetable oil. Add all the vegetables and fry for 2 minutes. Add the noodles and sauce, using a pair of tongs to make sure everything is completely coated in the sauce. Fry for 3–4 minutes, keeping everything moving in the pan. Serve sprinkled with the sesame seeds on top.

BUSAN-STYLE CHILLED NOODLES

밀면

MILMYEON

You might be familiar with the Korean cold noodles *naengmyeon*, which are eaten all over Korea and made from buckwheat to create a bouncy, chewy noodle served in an ice-cold broth. I love them, but I think I actually love these *milmyeon* noodles more. *Milmyeon* translates as 'wheat noodles' and were created during the Korean war. *Naengmyeon* traditionally comes from the Northern parts of Korea, where buckwheat is in abundance, but during the war, it was difficult to get hold of, particularly as many Koreans were forced towards the southern coast in and around Busan, where buckwheat was scarce. Craving these noodles, creative Koreans used the white flour available from American food rations and made *milmyeon* instead.

The broth is usually simmered for several hours, but this is a quick version for when I need to eat something cooling and refreshing for a speedy lunch.

200 g/7 oz. *somen* (thin wheat noodles)
600 ml/2½ cups cold beef stock
6 tbsp Korean apple/rice vinegar
4 tsp granulated sugar
2 tsp fish sauce
2 handfuls of ice (about 300 g/10½ oz.)

MOOLI RIBBONS
100 g/3½ oz. mooli, peeled
1½ tbsp Korean apple/rice vinegar
4 tsp granulated sugar
½ tsp *gochugaru* (Korean red pepper flakes)
½ tsp salt

DADAEGI SEASONING SAUCE
3 tbsp *gochugaru* (Korean red pepper flakes)
2 tbsp Korean apple/rice vinegar
1 tbsp granulated sugar
1 tbsp toasted sesame oil
1½ tbsp light soy sauce
½ tsp crushed/minced garlic

TO FINISH
cucumber, cut into thin strips
2 slices of roast beef (can be roast beef slices used for sandwiches), cut into thick strips
1 boiled egg, halved (optional)

SERVES 2

Cut the mooli into 5-cm/2-inch chunks and then use a peeler to keep peeling to create lots of thin ribbons. Place them in a bowl with the rest of the mooli ribbon ingredients, mix and set to one side.

In a small bowl, mix the *dadaegi* seasoning sauce ingredients and set to one side.

Fill a pan with water and bring to the boil. Add the noodles and boil for 3 minutes. Drain and rinse with cold water.

Divide the beef stock between two bowls and top each bowl with an extra 100 ml/scant ½ cup water. Season each bowl with 3 tablespoons of the vinegar, 2 teaspoons of the sugar and 1 teaspoon of the fish sauce. Divide the noodles between each bowl.

Crush the ice (or use a food processor to blitz it) and divide between the bowls. Top with the pickled mooli ribbons, cucumber, sliced beef, boiled egg, if using, and a little *dadaegi* seasoning sauce with more on the side to add extra seasoning if needed.

BEST BITS
FRIED RICE

베스트 볶음밥
BEST BOKKEUMBAP

Korean food is very much about sharing and when you go to a restaurant you normally order a big dish to place in the middle of the table, which comes with a selection of *banchan* (side dishes). If the main dish is cooked in a sauce – such as *ori bulgogi* (spicy duck in gochujang sauce) – then after everyone has eaten the meat, it's very common to ask for rice to be fried in the remaining sauce. Sometimes this is done at the table and sometimes the serving dish is taken away and it's prepared in the kitchen – but whichever way this fried rice is made, it is often the best part of the meal. This recipe recreates all of that flavour, including the best crispy bits of rice, without having to wait until everyone else has finished the meat part of the meal!

1 tbsp vegetable oil

150 g/5½ oz. pork belly, finely sliced

200 g/1½ cups cooked short-grain rice

2 tbsp toasted sesame oil

3 spring onions/scallions, finely chopped, plus a little extra to garnish

2 tsp crushed/minced garlic

½ tsp crushed/minced ginger

1½ tbsp *gochujang* (Korean red pepper paste)

1 tbsp Korean soy sauce

1½ tbsp light soft brown sugar

5-g/¼ oz. pack of salted snack seaweed

2 tbsp toasted sesame seeds

SERVES 2

Place a large frying pan/skillet over a high heat with the vegetable oil. Add the pork belly and fry for 3–4 minutes. Add the rice, sesame oil, spring onions, garlic, ginger, *gochujang*, soy sauce and sugar. Mix to make sure everything is coated in the sauce.

Using the back of a spoon, smooth out the rice to evenly cover the base of the pan to crisp up the bottom.

Reduce the heat to medium and leave for 3 minutes.

Stir the rice again, making sure to scrape up any crispy bits on the base of the pan. Crush up the seaweed in the packet and add it to the pan along with the sesame seeds. Garnish with the extra spring onion and enjoy!

KIMCHI & BACON FRIED RICE

When you need something tasty and satisfying, but only have 10 minutes, I don't think there's much better than kimchi fried rice. The bacon here gives a lovely smoky flavour that works really well with the kimchi, and it's a great way of using any leftover rice you might have sitting in the fridge. It's the kind of dish that is delicious both hot and cold, so it can be a quick midweek dinner (topped with a fried egg makes it even better), but also could be packed away in a container for a portable picnic lunch, too.

1 tbsp vegetable oil
100 g/3½ oz. smoked bacon
    lardons
200 g/7 oz. kimchi, drained
    and roughly chopped
250 g/1¾ cups cooked
    short-grain rice
1 tsp *gochujang*
    (Korean red pepper paste)
1 tbsp toasted sesame oil
1 spring onion/scallion, finely
    chopped
2 fried eggs, to serve (optional)

SERVES 2

Place a large frying pan/skillet over a high heat with the vegetable oil. Add the bacon lardons and fry for 2 minutes. Add the kimchi and fry for a further 2 minutes. Add the rice, *gochujang* and sesame oil. Fry for a further 2 minutes. Stir in the spring onions and serve, topped with a fried egg, if using.

TIP *If you're in a midweek rush, and you don't have any cooked rice to hand, you can use a packet of microwave rice here instead (ideally short grain, but any plain rice will do).*

KIMCHI WRAPS
WITH CHILLI BEEF

묵은지 김치 쌈
MOOKEUNJI KIMCHI SSAM

In Korea, the cabbages (Chinese leaves) for kimchi are best from around October, so we traditionally have *kimjang* where communities get together to make big batches of kimchi, which last throughout the very cold winter months and into the next year. Kimchi is more than a side dish in Korean food, it's also used as an ingredient in so many dishes, from *mandu* (dumplings) to *kimchi jeon* pancakes – and when it is very, very ripe, the whole cabbage kimchi can be washed and used to wrap rice as an alternative to *ssam* (lettuce wraps).

When I was little, we used to spend the whole of my summer holidays in Korea and we would visit my mum's high school friends. One of her friends knew that I loved this tangy washed kimchi, so would always make sure she kept some for our visits. I've got such strong memories of us all sitting together using these washed leaves to simply wrap spoonfuls of rice with a smear of *gochujang* (Korean red pepper paste) in the middle. Here, I've used *yak gochujang*, a beef and chilli spicy paste, for extra flavour, but even a simple smear of *gochujang* is great, too, when you're in more of a hurry.

2 store-bought whole cabbage
  kimchi (see page 16)
250 g/1¾ cups cooked sushi rice
toasted sesame seeds, to garnish

YAK GOCHUJANG
200 g/7 oz. minced/ground beef
1 spring onion/scallion, finely
  chopped
1 tbsp mirin
1 tbsp Korean soy sauce
½ tsp freshly ground black pepper
2 tbsp toasted sesame oil
1 tbsp vegetable oil
5 tbsp *gochujang*
  (Korean red pepper paste)
2½ tbsp honey
1 tsp crushed/minced garlic
1 tbsp toasted sesame seeds,
  plus extra to garnish

SERVES 2

Wash the cabbage kimchi thoroughly and squeeze out any excess water, then set aside.

In a medium bowl, mix together the beef, spring onion, mirin, soy sauce, black pepper and 1 tablespoon of the sesame oil.

Place a frying pan/skillet over a high heat, add the oil and fry the beef for 3 minutes. Add the *gochujang*, honey, garlic, sesame seeds and 3 tablespoons water. Reduce the heat to low and stir for 2 minutes. Stir in the remaining sesame oil to finish.

Lay a kimchi leaf on a chopping board and add a tablespoon of rice. Top with a teaspoon of the *yak gochujang* on top and roll into a little parcel. Repeat with the remaining kimchi leaves. Sprinkle with sesame seeds to finish.

DUMPLING
FRIED RICE

This is the recipe that I turn to when I need to make dinner in a hurry for my kids – they both love it and we usually have all the ingredients handy. It's a fantastic midweek dinner as it can be thrown together in minutes with hardly any chopping involved (you can just snip the spring onions/scallions quickly with a pair of scissors), so it's minimal washing up too! Use leftover rice (I often have some in the freezer) or packets of ready-cooked short grain/sushi rice to keep things easy.

1 tbsp vegetable oil
12 frozen *mandu* dumplings
  (about 240 g/8½ oz.)
1 carrot, grated/shredded
2 spring onions/scallions,
  finely chopped
1 tsp crushed/minced garlic
280 g/10 oz. cooked sushi rice
1½ tbsp Korean soy sauce
1½ tbsp toasted sesame oil
small handful of spinach
  (about 30 g/¾ cup)
kimchi, to serve

SERVES 2

Place a large frying pan/skillet over a medium-high heat with the vegetable oil. Add the frozen dumplings, carrot, spring onions and garlic and fry for 5 minutes, breaking up the *mandu* with a pair of tongs or scissors as they start to defrost and soften.

Add the rice and soy sauce and fry for 2 minutes, stirring to make sure the rice and *mandu* don't catch at the bottom of the pan.

Add the sesame oil and spinach and continue to stir for 1 minute until the spinach is wilted.

Serve and enjoy with a side of kimchi.

TIP *The flavour of this dish changes depending on which* mandu *you have. I usually use pork dumplings, which give the dish quite a subtle flavour, but bulgogi beef dumplings add a delicious soy sauce salty sweetness, which gives this dish a whole new dimension, so choose whichever* mandu *you love most!*

VEG

야채

A FEW YEARS AGO, I WAS LUCKY ENOUGH TO BE SPONSORED BY THE KOREAN TOURISM ORGANIZATION AND THE GUILD OF FOOD WRITERS TO GO TO KOREA AND EXPLORE KOREAN TEMPLE CUISINE. I had wanted to find out more about this area of Korean food as I had attended an online masterclass with revered monk Jeong Kwan sunim and found the ideas behind Korean temple food really interesting.

Korean temple food is completely plant based, so it showcases a different side to Korean food, which is so often associated with meat and BBQ. It's also fascinating, because they do not use the five pungent vegetables of garlic, leeks, onions, spring onions/scallions and chives, which are all synonymous with Korean cuisine. Instead, flavour is elevated by using simple seasonal ingredients and slow fermentation.

During my trip, I attended a temple stay at Baekyangsa Temple where I enjoyed monastic meals, Buddhist prayer and tea in the beautiful surroundings of Naejangsan National Park. The highlight of the stay though was attending a cookery workshop, where I had the opportunity to watch and learn from Jeong Kwan sunim in person. As we walked up to her kitchen, we could see the earthenware *onngi* pots just outside, which stored *gochujang* (Korean red pepper paste), *doenjang* (fermented soy bean paste) and soy sauce of various ages that are made on site. As we stepped inside, it was incredible to hear her speak about the relationship between the food you eat and the impact this has on your body and mind, how healing food can be and the philosophies behind temple cuisine. Food and health are very much linked in Korean cooking and culture, with the idea that contrasting flavours and colours bring more than just beautiful presentation to a meal, but actually nourish the body from the inside out, and temple cuisine really takes this to another level. We enjoyed an amazing spread of dishes as Jeong Kwan sunim detailed the different ingredients, methods of food preservation and cooking techniques she uses to get the most out of the freshly grown produce.

I've always been a big meat eater, but nowadays I'm a little more conscious of eating less meat and more vegetables. I still love alliums so this section isn't completely about temple food, but some of the recipes were inspired by my trip to Baekyangsa Temple and others are just delicious meat alternatives that we love to eat at home. My kids both love tofu, so these are the recipes we probably eat the most often – I know that tofu might not be for everyone, but I believe that it's all down to how it is cooked, and so I hope that some of these recipes might convert you if you're not already a big fan!

TOFU & CHILLI FRITTERS

두부고추전
DUBU GOCHU JEON

These 'fritters' are actually more like vegetarian meatballs. They're shaped into small patties and have a real umami depth to them because of the *doenjang* (soy bean paste), which gives a deliciously spicy chilli kick.

A few years ago, I attended a cooking class at Baekyangsa Temple in Korea (see page 134). It was a great opportunity to learn more about Korean temple food, and I was surprised by the use of chilli in the Buddhist kitchen. I knew that alliums were avoided and had thought that temple food would be much plainer and neutral in flavour, but it was really interesting to see how Korean Buddhist temple cuisine really makes the most of fresh ingredients to ensure that the food is flavourful even without the use of garlic or onions, which are so often found in Korean cuisine.

150 g/5½ oz. firm tofu
1 long red chilli/chile, finely chopped
2½ tbsp plain/all-purpose flour
¼ tsp baking powder
2 tsp *doenjang*
   (Korean soy bean paste)
1 tsp *gochujang*
   (Korean red pepper paste)
1 tbsp vegetable oil
chopped spring onions/scallions,
   to garnish

MAKES 8 FRITTERS

Drain the tofu, squeeze out any excess water and crumble into a large mixing bowl. Add the rest of the ingredients, except the oil, along with 1 tablespoon water and mix together.

Shape the mixture into 8 evenly sized balls, squeezing into small patties and gently flatten to 1 cm/½ inch thick.

Heat the oil in a large frying pan/skillet over a medium-low heat. Add the tofu patties and fry for 3 minutes until golden. Flip and fry for another 2 minutes. These can be eaten hot or cold, garnished with chopped spring onions.

TIP *These can be eaten as a banchan (side dish) with rice (pick your favourites), on their own as a snack for lunch and also make a great sandwich filling with some salad and gochujang sauce.*

SPICY BRAISED TOFU

두부찜
DUBU JJIM

This is another dish that I have often – it's great for lunch or dinner and really only takes minutes to make. The frying step is actually optional – it gives the tofu more bite and when I cooked this dish for a cookery class, the class was split, with a few preferring the texture of the fried version. At home though, I often skip this step and simply put the tofu straight into the pan with the sauce and simmer for a silkier, softer tofu, but I've included the frying step here in case you prefer your tofu to have more texture.

800 g/1¾ lb. firm tofu
pinch of salt
1 tbsp vegetable oil
½ onion, sliced
½ long red chilli/chile, sliced
1 spring onion/scallion,
    roughly chopped
freshly steamed rice, to serve

SAUCE
3 tbsp Korean soy sauce
1 tbsp *gochugaru*
    (Korean red pepper flakes)
1 tbsp mirin
1 tbsp toasted sesame oil
1½ tsp caster/superfine sugar
1 tsp crushed/minced garlic
¼ tsp ground white pepper

SERVES 2

Place the tofu onto a plate and rest another plate on top. Place something heavy on top and leave for about 10 minutes to squeeze out all the extra water from the tofu.

Meanwhile, mix together the sauce ingredients with 150 ml/⅔ cup water in a small bowl.

Pat the tofu dry and then slice into large rectangles, around 1 cm/½ inch thick. Season with the salt

Place a large frying pan/skillet over a medium-high heat with the vegetable oil. Carefully lay the tofu into the pan and fry on each side for 2 minutes.

Add the onion, chilli, spring onion (saving some of the green part for garnishing) and sauce. Bring to the boil, and then reduce the heat to a simmer for 10 minutes.

Serve garnished with spring onions and with freshly steamed rice.

CLEVER POTATO PANCAKES

감자전

GAMJA JEON

These potato pancakes are crisp on the outside with a slightly chewy middle. They are vegan, gluten free and the clever thing about them is that they create their own starch, so no additional flour is needed. After blending the potatoes, the purée is left to sit in a sieve/strainer to remove any excess liquid, leaving a white potato starch paste, which helps to make the potatoes crispy and bind together – it really is the magic ingredient so make sure not to pour this away!

500 g/1 lb. 2 oz. floury potatoes, left unpeeled and roughly chopped
¼ onion, roughly chopped
½ tsp salt
1 red chilli/chile, finely sliced
vegetable oil, for frying

SAUCE
1 red chilli/chile, sliced
1 green chilli/chile, sliced
4 tbsp Korean soy sauce
2 tbsp Korean apple/rice vinegar
pinch of toasted sesame seeds

MAKES 9 PANCAKES

Place the potatoes, onion and salt in a food processor or blender along with 100 ml/scant ½ cup water and blend until smooth. Place a sieve/strainer over a bowl, pour in the puréed potato and leave for 10 minutes.

Meanwhile, mix the chillies with the soy sauce, vinegar and sesame seeds to make the sauce and leave to one side.

Lift the sieve with the puréed potato off the bowl and set to one side.

Slowly pour away the drained water, making sure to keep the white paste stuck to the bottom of the bowl. Scrape the white paste with a spoon to loosen. Add the potato purée into the bowl and mix with the starch.

Place a non-stick frying pan/skillet over a high heat with 1 tablespoon vegetable oil. Add 1 tablespoon of the potato mixture, then flatten and smooth the top of the pancake with the back of a spoon so that the pancake is about 5 mm/¼ inch thick. Press a chilli slice on the top of each pancake.

Leaving some space, spoon more mixture onto the pan and repeat so that there are 3 pancakes in the pan. Fry for 1½ minutes, then carefully flip and fry for a further 1½ minutes. Drain on paper towels.

Repeat the frying method for the remaining potato mixture, adding another tablespoon vegetable oil for each batch of pancakes.

Serve immediately with the dipping sauce.

TIP *If you do accidentally throw away the white potato starch, mix in a tablespoon of potato starch flour or cornflour/cornstarch instead.*

STICKY TOFU RICE BOWL WITH PICKLED CARROT

두부덮밥
DUBU DUP BAP

This is one of our family favourites, particularly with my kids – and even though we are a big meat-eating household, I promise that the crunchy little nuggets of tofu coated in that sweet, salty, sticky sauce are completely irresistible. My kids love the pickled carrots too. I usually cut the carrots into rounds to keep things quick during the week, but you could also slice them into thin strips, peel them or use a little cutter to cut them into different shapes. Finish with any other vegetables that you and your family like – I usually serve it with cucumber slices for a little freshness and extra crunch.

400 g/14 oz. firm tofu, drained
1 tbsp Korean soy sauce
2 tsp toasted sesame seeds
2 tsp cornflour/cornstarch
1 tsp toasted sesame oil
¼ tsp freshly ground black pepper
300 g/10½ oz. freshly cooked
    short-grain rice, to serve
cucumber or other green veg,
    to serve

PICKLED CARROTS
2 tbsp granulated sugar
4 tbsp Korean apple/rice vinegar
1 carrot, cut into 5-mm/¼-inch
    rounds or other shapes

SAUCE
2 spring onions/scallions,
    finely chopped
2 tbsp Korean soy sauce
2 tbsp honey
2 tsp toasted sesame oil
½ tsp crushed/minced garlic

SERVES 2

First make the pickled carrots. In a small bowl, mix together the sugar, vinegar and 4 tablespoons water. Add the sliced carrot and coat in the pickling liquid and set to one side.

Break the tofu into small pieces and then squeeze out any excess water. Crumble the tofu into a medium-sized bowl and mix in the soy sauce, sesame seeds, cornflour, sesame oil and black pepper.

Spread evenly on a baking sheet and place in an air fryer at 180°C/350°F (see tip below for oven cooking instructions) for 8 minutes. Use a spoon to break up the tofu and flip it over and cook for another 3 minutes.

In a small bowl, mix together the sauce ingredients. Place a large frying pan/skillet over a high heat. Add the sauce and tofu and cook for about 2 minutes until the sauce is sticky and reduced.

Divide the rice into two bowls. Top with the tofu and pickled carrots and any additional green vegetables as liked.

TIP *If using an oven, increase the temperature to 190°C/170°C fan/ 375°F/Gas 5 and cook for 20 minutes, making sure to flip the tofu and break it up after 10 minutes.*

TOFU WITH SOY SPRING ONION DRESSING

My mum would often make this simple tofu *banchan* at home. When I was little, I wasn't a huge fan of plain tofu (and would always try and pinch the pieces coated in the most dressing), but nowadays I love the contrast of the almost neutral flavour of the tofu with the salty soy sauce. I can easily eat this tofu everyday – I've boiled it here, but you could also microwave it on a plate without any water for 2–3 minutes until heated through. Or on warmer days, I eat this cold with the tofu straight from the fridge and the dressing spooned on top.

¼ tsp salt
400 g/14 oz. firm tofu, drained

DRESSING
3 spring onions/scallions,
   finely chopped
2 tbsp Korean soy sauce
2 tbsp toasted sesame oil
1 tbsp toasted sesame seeds
1½ tsp *gochugaru*
   (Korean red pepper flakes)
¼ tsp crushed/minced garlic

SERVES 2–4 AS A BANCHAN

In a small bowl, mix together all the dressing ingredients with 1 tablespoon water and set aside.

Place a saucepan filled with water and the salt over a high heat. Once boiling, carefully place the tofu in the saucepan and boil for 5 minutes.

Using a pair of tongs, gently lift the tofu out of the water and place on a plate or board. Pat dry with paper towels. Slice the tofu block in half and then into 5-mm/¼-inch slices.

Lay the tofu slices on a plate and spoon the dressing carefully over the centre of the tofu.

TIP *This is usually served as a banchan side dish, but I also like to eat it on its own as a quick breakfast.*

ROASTED SWEET POTATO

군고구마
GUN-GOGUMA

Gun-goguma (roasted sweet potatoes) are a traditional street-food snack in Korea. My favourite memories are in Nampodong, Busan, where the street sellers push huge charcoal ovens to roast the sweet potatoes and you buy them by the bag. On my eldest's first trip to Korea, he insisted we buy a bag, and I remember that there wasn't anywhere nearby to sit and eat them, but being only little, he was impatient to try them as soon as possible. So, he and my mum sat on a kerb to peel the tops off and enjoy the hot sweet potato inside. This is how we often eat roasted sweet potatoes in Korea, by peeling the top half and then leaving the skin on the bottom half to hold so that your fingers don't get sticky.

Roasted sweet potatoes are also great topped with kimchi as it provides a lovely cool, tangy contrast to the piping hot, sweet flesh. My mum now often makes a batch in her oven to snack on during the day.

1 kg/2¼ lb. sweet potatoes
kimchi, to serve (optional)

SERVES 2–4 AS A SNACK

Preheat the oven to 180°C/160°C fan/350°F/Gas 4.

Wash the sweet potatoes and then prick holes liberally over each one with a fork.

Place the potatoes on a lined baking sheet and bake in the oven for 45–60 minutes, depending on their size. The sweet potatoes are ready when they start to seep sticky, caramelly liquid out of the pierced holes and are soft inside.

These can be eaten hot or cold. Peel the top half to bite into and use the bottom half with the skin as a handle.

Top with kimchi or eat on its own.

간장 드레싱 샐러드
GANJANG DRESSING SALAD

SOY SESAME SALAD

This is our go-to salad at home. I'm confident that I could toss any leaves/vegetables in this tasty dressing and my kids would still love it, but this is our usual combination.

150 g/5½ oz. baby plum tomatoes, halved
¼ tsp salt
1 carrot, grated/shredded
2 pickled beetroot/beet, quartered
¼ red cabbage, finely sliced
3 spring onions/scallions, finely chopped
1 apple, cored and finely sliced (skin on)
1 Little Gem/sweetheart lettuce, finely sliced

CROUTONS
2 slices of white bread, cut into 1-cm/½-inch cubes
1 tbsp toasted sesame seeds
2 tsp toasted sesame oil
1 tsp garlic granules
¼ tsp salt

DRESSING
3 tbsp Korean apple/rice vinegar
3 tbsp Korean soy sauce
1 tbsp toasted sesame oil
2 tbsp toasted sesame seeds
1 tbsp granulated sugar
½ tsp crushed/minced garlic

SERVES 4

Mix the dressing in a small bowl and set to one side.

Preheat the oven to 180°C/160°C fan/350°F/Gas 4.

For the croutons, mix the bread with the sesame seeds, sesame oil, garlic granules and salt. Spread the croutons out on a lined baking sheet in an even layer and bake in the oven for 10 minutes.

Place the tomatoes in a bowl, mix with the salt and set to one side for 5 minutes.

Place the carrot, beetroot, cabbage, spring onions and apple in a dish. Drain the tomatoes and add them to the dish. Add the lettuce and mix in the dressing. Scatter over the croutons to finish.

매운 드레싱 샐러드
MAEUN DRESSING SALAD

CRUNCHY CHILLI SALAD

The dressing on this salad is usually used on *pajeori*, a spring onion/scallion salad that is often eaten with Korean BBQ, but it works so well with crunchy vegetables and really brings a salad to life with its zingy, sweet chilli dressing. It's my favourite side dish for when we have friends over for a summer BBQ, as the tangy spice perfectly balances any barbecued meats.

¼ white cabbage, finely sliced or shredded
1 Little Gem lettuce, finely sliced
1 apple, finely sliced (skin on)
100 g/3½ oz. radishes, finely sliced
25 g/½ cup spinach, roughly chopped
1 tbsp *gochugaru* (Korean red pepper flakes)
1½ tbsp Korean apple/rice vinegar
2 tsp toasted sesame oil
1 tbsp caster/granulated sugar
1 tbsp toasted sesame seeds

SERVES 4

Put all the chopped ingredients into a large bowl and mix in the *gochugaru*, vinegar, sesame oil and sugar until everything is coated in the dressing.

Top with sesame seeds to serve.

STICKY, CRISPY FRIED MUSHROOMS

These are not *twigim* tempura in the traditional street-food sense, but instead the mushrooms are fried in a super light batter and then coated in a sweet, sticky glaze. The idea came about after my stay at Baekyangsa Temple in Korea, where we had the chance to watch revered monk, Jeong Kwan sunim, cook several different temple cuisine dishes. Rather than using sugar for sweetness, temple cuisine uses a lot of *cheong*, which are fruit syrups made from equal weights of fruit and sugar. When I had the idea for this dish, I didn't have any *cheong* to hand, so I used some orange marmalade that I had in the fridge and the citrusy sweetness worked so well with the crispy mushrooms that the recipe stuck!

3 tbsp vegetable oil
100 g/3½ oz. oyster mushrooms, roughly torn
1 green chilli/chile, finely sliced, to garnish
freshly steamed rice, to serve

BATTER
4 tbsp plain/all-purpose flour
3 tbsp cornflour/cornstarch
½ tsp freshly ground black pepper
¼ tsp salt

SAUCE
2 tbsp Korean soy sauce
1 tbsp toasted sesame oil
1 tbsp rice syrup
   (or agave/maple syrup)
1 tbsp orange marmalade (no peel)

SERVES 2 AS A BANCHAN

Mix the batter ingredients with 150 ml/⅔ cup water in a large bowl.

Heat the vegetable oil in a large frying pan/skillet over a high heat (until you can drop a little batter in and it sizzles).

Lightly coat each piece of mushroom in the batter and gently place them in the pan, making sure they have enough space so that they don't stick together. You may need to cook them in batches depending on the size of your pan. Fry for 3 minutes until crispy, then remove from the pan and drain on paper towels.

Heat the sauce ingredients together in a saucepan over a medium heat until the jam melts into the rest of the sauce. Add the crispy mushrooms and lightly coat in the sauce.

Serve immediately and garnish with the green chilli.

HEARTY SOY
BEAN STEW

If you're already familiar with Korean food, you might have tried *doenjang jjigae*, which is a stew made from Korean fermented soy bean paste. *Gang doenjang* is a thickened stew and is a concentrated version of *doenjang jjigae*. It is saltier, richer and heartier, making it a perfect filling for steamed cabbage leaves. As the flavours are much more intense, always eat this with rice – either in a cabbage or lettuce wrap, or even as a *bibimbap* by mixing a few spoonfuls of *gang doenjang* into freshly steamed rice for a super speedy meal.

1 tbsp vegetable oil
½ courgette/zucchini,
    finely chopped
1 onion, finely chopped
2 tbsp *doenjang*
    (Korean soy bean paste)
1 tsp *gochujang*
    (Korean red pepper paste)
200 g/7 oz. firm tofu, drained and
    cut into 5-mm/¼-inch cubes
½ red chilli/chile, finely sliced
2 spring onions/scallions,
    finely chopped
½ cabbage
freshly steamed rice, to serve

SERVES 2

Place a saucepan over a medium-high heat with the vegetable oil. Add the courgette and onion and fry for 4–5 minutes until softened and the onion is translucent.

Stir in the *doenjang* and *gochujang* and fry for 1 minute, making sure everything is coated well. Mix in the tofu, chilli and half the spring onions. Pour in 100 ml/scant ½ cup water and bring to the boil, reduce to a simmer and cook for 10 minutes.

Meanwhile, bring a large pan of water to the boil. Separate the cabbage leaves and drop them in the pan. Cover with a lid and blanch for about 5 minutes until softened. Drain the cabbage leaves, rinse under cold water and set to one side.

Top with the remaining spring onions and serve immediately with the cabbage leaves and some freshly steamed rice.

SPICY BRAISED MOOLI

I often think of Korean radish (or the more easily accessible mooli) as a bit of a 'flavour sponge'. It really soaks up the flavours of any dish and is often found in braises and stews in Korea. When I was younger, my mum would often make *godeunga jorim*, a spicy braised mackerel with mooli. The mackerel is obviously meant to be the star of the show, but it's the mooli that really takes on all the flavour and is what we call in Korean, a *bap doddeuk*, or 'rice thief', as you just want more and more rice to eat it with to soak up the sauce. This recipe is packed full of lots of flavour but is quicker and easier to throw together with minimal prep needed.

8 tbsp Korean soy sauce
3 tbsp *gochugaru*
    (Korean red pepper flakes)
2 tbsp caster/superfine sugar
2 tsp crushed/minced garlic
1 Korean radish or mooli (weighing
    about 750 g/1 lb. 10 oz.), peeled,
    sliced in half lengthways and then
    into 1-cm/½-inch thick slices
700 ml/3 cups Anchovy Stock
    (see page 90), or same amount
    of water mixed with 1 tsp dashi
    powder
2 tsp toasted sesame oil
1 spring onion/scallion, finely
    chopped
freshly steamed rice, to serve

SERVES 4

In a small bowl, mix together the soy sauce, *gochugaru*, sugar and garlic, then set aside.

In a large saucepan, bring the anchovy stock (or water with dashi powder) to the boil over a high heat. Add the mooli and sauce and boil for about 20 minutes until the mooli has softened.

Finish with the sesame oil and spring onion and serve with freshly steamed rice.

SPICY MUSHROOM HOTPOT

A *jeongol* (hot pot or stew) is a sharing dish and I think of this one as a real celebration of mushrooms. There are lots of different types of *jeongol* in Korea, but they always have a variety of different vegetables for texture, colour and flavour as they're usually presented in the middle of the table, over a little gas stove to finish cooking and everyone helps themselves to (several) piping hot bowlfuls.

This *jeongol* has a real fiery kick and is packed with so much flavour, but also happens to be vegan too. Serve it with individual portions of rice to balance out the spicy heat, but at the end you can add instant ramen noodles (without the seasoning packet) or udon to soak up the last of the broth – simply bring the remaining broth up to the boil and add the noodles for 3–4 minutes until just cooked.

2 portobello mushrooms,
 thinly sliced
1 tbsp Korean soy sauce
1 tsp crushed/minced garlic
½ tsp freshly ground black pepper
1 tbsp vegetable oil
150 g/5½ oz. chestnut mushrooms,
 cut into 5-mm/¼-inch slices
 (leave a handful for decoration)
150 g/5½ oz. button mushrooms,
 cut into quarters
85 g/3 oz. oyster mushrooms,
 roughly torn
5 spring onions/scallions,
 cut into 5-cm/2-inch lengths
1 carrot, cut into batons

SAUCE
3 tbsp *gochugaru*
 (Korean red pepper flakes)
2½ tbsp light soy sauce
2 tbsp mirin
1 tbsp crushed/minced garlic
½ tsp freshly ground black pepper
¼ tsp salt

SERVES 4

Mix together the sauce ingredients in a small bowl and set to one side.

Place the sliced portobello mushrooms in a bowl with the soy sauce, garlic and black pepper. Squeeze the mushrooms so they take on all the flavour, then drain off any excess liquid.

Place a hot pot dish or shallow casserole over a high heat with the vegetable oil. Fry the portobello mushrooms for 5 minutes until there's no liquid left in the bottom of the dish. Remove the portobello mushrooms and set to one side.

Fill the pan with 700 ml/scant 3 cups water and the sauce and bring to the boil. Once boiling, reduce the heat to medium and arrange the remaining mushrooms, spring onions and carrot on top, in an alternating pattern. Place the fried portobello mushrooms in the middle.

Bring the pan back to the boil and cook for 4–5 minutes until all the mushrooms are cooked.

SWEET
TREATS
디저트

IN THE PAST, I WOULD HAVE SAID THAT DESSERTS WERE NOT A
HUGE THING IN KOREA AS WE DON'T OFTEN EAT THEM AT THE END
OF A MEAL – and if we do, it is usually in the form of sliced fresh fruit served
in the middle of the table to share.

However, sweet treats are often eaten on their own, separate to a meal
or given on celebratory occasions as gifts, especially rice cakes, which are often
beautifully presented in an assortment of different colours and are particularly
popular at *Chuseok* (Korean Thanksgiving). They are also one of the important
dishes offered as part of *charye* (ancestral memorials), when specific dishes are
offered to the spirits of those that have passed away.

Rather than being eaten as a dessert after a meal, sweet treats are enjoyed
at any time of the day and the scent of the sweet, buttery *hotteok* (cinnamon
sugar filled pancakes) and *bungeobbang* (fish shaped waffles filled with
sweetened red bean paste) fills the air at any street-food market. There are
hundreds of ice cream shops open until late, and dessert cafés and bakeries
can be found everywhere, with the most delicious array of cakes, pastries and
bingsu (Korean shaved ice) on offer.

Coffee culture has also become huge in Korea, and there are so many
beautiful independent coffee shops and thousands of well-known coffee chains.
In fact, it was reported in 2023 that there were almost 100,000 coffee shops
in Korea and everywhere you go, there's always a new, trendy one opening. A few
years ago, this love of coffee made its way to social media as *dalgona* iced coffee
became a huge trend. Since it's such an easy recipe and my absolute go-to in the
summer, I had to include the recipe here, too.

I have a really sweet tooth and can't resist a little treat, so I've included some
of my favourites in this chapter – there's traditional like the *hwachae* (fruit punch),
those with a twist like my easy *hotteok*, and then there's the *doenjang* and white
chocolate cookies, which take Korean flavours but in a whole new way, which I
hope you'll love.

DOENJANG & WHITE CHOCOLATE COOKIES

I sometimes think that *doenjang* is under-appreciated, maybe because 'fermented soy bean', sounds quite unappealing? Here, the salty, earthiness of the *doenjang* is balanced by the sweet white chocolate to make the perfect cookie.

100 g/½ cup/1 stick softened unsalted butter
120 g/⅔ cup golden caster/superfine sugar
2 tsp *doenjang* (Korean soy bean paste)
200 g/1½ cups plain/all-purpose flour
1 tsp baking powder
½ tsp bicarbonate of soda/baking soda
50 ml/3½ tbsp milk
100 g/3½ oz. white chocolate, broken
　　into small chunks

MAKES 9 COOKIES

Preheat the oven to 180°C/160°C fan/350°F/Gas 4 and line a baking sheet with baking paper.

In a large bowl (or stand mixer), cream together the butter, sugar and *doenjang*. Add the flour, baking powder and bicarbonate of soda. Mix with a wooden spoon and add the milk. The mixture will look a little crumbly at first but it will start sticking together. Add the white chocolate and use your fingers to bring the dough together.

Shape the dough into small balls (about 60 g/2 oz. each). Place the dough balls on the baking sheet, making sure to give each plenty of space. Bake in the oven for 14–15 minutes until the edges are golden. Leave to cool on the tray. Enjoy with a *dalgona* iced coffee!

TIP *If you have time, place the cookie dough in the fridge for an hour before baking.*

DALGONA ICE COFFEE

If you're active on social media, you might have seen *dalgona* coffee before, but I had to include it here because it is so delicious and easy to make – I have one almost daily in the summer. *Dalgona* refers to a street food (sometimes also called *bbopkki*) made from sugar and baking powder, which sets into a thin, crisp honeycomb – made famous on the Netflix show, *Squid Game*. This delicious and refreshing iced coffee is named after this street food treat, because of its sweet, caramel flavour that's hard to resist.

1 tbsp instant coffee granules
2 tsp light soft brown sugar
1½ tbsp boiling water
2 handfuls of ice
200 ml/scant 1 cup milk (of your choice)

SERVES 1

Spoon the coffee and sugar into a highball glass. Add the boiling water on top and use an electric milk frother to mix it all together for 10–15 seconds until the coffee has doubled in volume.

Fill the glass with ice cubes and top with milk. Give everything a gentle stir and enjoy!

TIP *If you don't have an electric milk frother, mix the coffee, sugar and boiling water in a large bowl with a whisk first, then spoon the coffee mixture into the glass. This is how I used to make them, but a little milk frother makes things much easier (and less washing up!).*

WATERMELON PUNCH

I don't remember having many desserts growing up, but I do have fond memories of my mum making this *subak hwachae* in the summer. Thinking back, I think she used to make a very simple version by chopping the watermelon into bite-sized pieces, sprinkling lots of sugar on top and adding ice. Such a fantastic summer treat! I've added mango to this version for extra flavour and colour, and some homemade *tteok* (rice cake balls). If you like bubble tea, you'll love these as the squishy little balls add a similar jelly-like texture. For the juice, I've just used water here, but if you'd like to make things extra fancy, you can swap this out for sparkling water instead, which makes it feel even more special!

¼ watermelon
(about 600 g/1 lb. 5 oz.)
¼ mango
ice cubes, to serve

JUICE
100 g/½ cup caster/superfine sugar
⅛ watermelon (about 300 g/10½ oz.), roughly chopped

TTEOK/RICE CAKE BALLS (OPTIONAL)
4 tbsp glutinous (sweet) rice flour
pinch of salt
1 tsp caster/superfine sugar
3 tbsp boiling water

SERVES 4

First make a sugar syrup that will be used in the juice. Put the sugar in a pan with 100 ml/scant ½ cup water over a medium heat. Bring to a simmer and stir until the sugar has dissolved and reduced to make a syrup (takes about 1–2 minutes). Leave to cool.

To make the *tteok* rice cake balls, mix the rice flour, salt and sugar together in a medium-sized bowl. Add the water and mix with a spoon. Once cool enough to handle, roll into a sausage shape and break off small segments to roll into marble-sized balls. If the dough starts to dry out and crumble, add a couple of drops of water to the balls when rolling.

Bring a pan of water to the boil. Carefully drop the rice cake balls into the boiling water. Give them an occasional stir to make sure they don't stick together. Drain, rinse and place in a bowl of cold water. Set to one side.

Cut the watermelon and mango into bite-sized pieces. You can do this with a knife by just cutting into cubes or use a melon baller to get a spherical shape. If using a melon baller, keep any remaining watermelon to add to the juice later. Place the cut/balled fruit into a large bowl.

To make the juice, blitz the watermelon for the juice, along with any remaining watermelon from making the watermelon balls, in a food processor. Pass the liquid through a sieve/strainer over the bowl of cut watermelon and mango. Add the sugar syrup and cooled *tteok* balls. Chill in the fridge for at least 30 minutes. When ready, serve with plenty of ice.

CINNAMON SUGAR PANCAKES

호떡

HOTTEOK

Hotteok are filled pancakes that are light, fluffy and cooked in lots of butter. I always describe them as a bit of a cross between a doughnut and a pancake because they're so much more than just a plain pancake. Inside, they're filled with lots of brown sugar, which becomes molten once they're fried, creating an oozy, caramel centre. They are a popular street-food snack in Korea, and particularly famous in Busan where they're often filled with seeds as well as sugar. They are usually made with a yeasted dough, which you'd have to wait to rise, so I created this cheat's version that can be made quickly for a weekend breakfast treat!

220 g/1⅔ cups plain/all-purpose
    flour, plus extra for dusting
1½ tsp baking powder
170 g/¾ cup natural/plain yogurt
3 tbsp salted butter

FILLING
5 tbsp dark soft brown sugar
1½ tbsp mixed seeds,
    roughly crushed
½ tsp ground cinnamon
pinch of salt

MAKES 8 PANCAKES

Mix together the filling ingredients in a small bowl and set to one side.

In a large mixing bowl, mix together the flour, baking powder and yogurt with a spoon until the mixture starts to come together as a dough. Use your hands to form a ball of dough and knead for 5 minutes until smooth. Split the dough into 8 evenly sized pieces and roll each piece into a ball.

Taking one dough ball at a time, flatten the dough in the palm of your hand to create a circle, using an extra pinch of flour if the dough begins to stick to your hands. Take a big pinch of the filling (about 1½ teaspoons) and place in the centre of the flattened dough. Fold the edges of the dough into the centre, overlapping a little to seal in the filling. Flatten in between both hands until it is about 1 cm/½ inch thick. Repeat with the remaining dough balls.

Place a large non-stick frying pan/skillet over a medium heat with 1½ tablespoons of the butter. Once the butter has melted, place 4 of the pancakes into the pan, evenly spaced.

Fry for 2 minutes until golden, flip each pancake and then place a lid over the top to steam them. Cook for a further 2 minutes. Remove the first 4 pancakes and set to one side.

Clean the pan using some kitchen paper, then place it back onto the stove over a medium heat with the remaining butter. Repeat the cooking process for the remaining dough balls.

Serve and eat immediately, being careful of the molten caramel filling!

TIP *This is even better when you slice the pancake horizontally and serve with a scoop of ice cream in the middle.*

BROWN SUGAR & SESAME RICE CAKES

흑설탕 떡
HEUK SEULTANG TTEOK

Growing up, sweet *tteok* rice cakes were never my favourite dessert, but nowadays they hold a special nostalgia for me and I love them. My youngest is a huge, huge fan of rice cakes (both savoury and sweet) – I think there's something about their unique chew that he adores. This recipe is by no means traditional, but it is quick and perfect for when you have that sweet craving – especially if you have a handful of rice cakes left over from another recipe. *Tteok* rice cakes are usually gifted and eaten on celebratory occasions in Korea, but this recipe means you can make a special treat in less than 5 minutes, any day of the week.

250 g/9 oz. *garae tteok*
  (long cylindrical rice cakes)

TO COAT
4 tbsp light soft brown sugar
2 tbsp toasted sesame seeds
¼ tsp salt

SERVES 2

Place a saucepan filled with water over a high heat. Bring to the boil and add the rice cakes. Boil for 2½ minutes until softened.

Meanwhile, spread the sugar, sesame seeds and salt over a plate.

Drain the rice cakes and rinse under cold water. Shake them dry.

Roll the rice cakes in the sesame sugar mixture until coated. It's easiest to do this one by one. These are best eaten immediately!

TIP *Use toasted sesame seeds in this recipe to get the best flavour and nutty fragrance and demerara/raw sugar gives the coating a lovely sweet crunch if you prefer, making it the perfect sweet treat to enjoy alongside a cup of coffee.*

STRAWBERRY SHAVED ICE

I love *bingsu* (shaved ice). There is nothing that cools you down faster in the summer than this dessert. Traditionally, *bingsu* started as a crushed ice dessert, topped with *pat* (sweetened red bean), which is still popular in Korea. However, these days, instead of just ice made from water, *bingsu* is usually made from very soft, milky snow-like flakes, topped with fruit and condensed milk. My favourite toppings are either strawberry or mango, but you could top this with whatever sweet, ripe fruit you like.

500 ml/2 cups whole/full-fat milk
5 tbsp condensed milk
1 scoop of vanilla ice cream
   (optional)
5 strawberries, halved

SERVES 2

Freeze the milk in ice cube trays – I find it easiest to use silicone ones here. Leave for 6 hours or overnight until completely solid.

Using a grating attachment on a food processor, drop the milky ice cubes in and grate on full power until they become a fine snow.

Spoon 2 tablespoons of the condensed milk into a bowl and tip the *bingsu* mixture on top.

Top with ice cream, if using, and decorate with the strawberry halves. Pour the remaining condensed milk on top and serve immediately.

TIPS *If you don't have a food processor, you could freeze the milk in a plastic container instead and grate the ice block by hand.*

You can also buy vegan condensed milk these days and do substitute the milk for any plant-based alternative to make this dairy free if needed.

STRAWBERRY CREAM (PAN) CAKE

DDALGI CREAM CAKE

Over the last few years, there's been a real explosion of bakeries and cute coffee shops in Korea and I always love visiting them when I'm there. As you enter, you usually pick up a lined tray and then wander around all the sweetly scented cakes and pastries, laden your tray with all the delicious treats and then pay at the counter before sitting down and devouring your haul.

One of the things that really stands out about Korean cakes is that they're usually very light and generously filled and/or covered with plenty of cream. I wanted to be able to replicate this at home, but without the hassle and time of waiting for lots of cakes to bake in the oven – so I came up with this frying pan/skillet solution! The cakes come out very thin, like a pancake, but are light, sweet and airy – perfect for layering with plenty of cream and fruit – and much quicker than cooking it in the oven! I've used strawberries here, but any berries, cherries or sliced ripe plums would also be delicious!

180 g/1⅓ cups plain/all-purpose flour
1 tsp baking powder
¼ tsp salt
100 g/½ cup granulated sugar
5 tbsp vegetable oil, plus extra for greasing
180 ml/¾ cup lemonade
2 tsp vanilla extract
2 tsp white vinegar

FILLING
400 ml/1⅔ cups double/heavy cream
3 tbsp icing/powdered sugar, plus extra to finish
1 tsp vanilla extract
600 g/1 lb. 5 oz. strawberries, hulled and cut in half

piping/pastry bag

SERVES 4

In a large bowl, mix together the flour, baking powder, salt and sugar. Add the vegetable oil, lemonade, vanilla extract and vinegar to the middle of the dry mixture and whisk to combine all the ingredients.

In a separate large bowl, whisk together the cream, icing sugar and vanilla extract. This is easiest with an electric whisk or stand mixer as the cream filling needs to be stiff enough to hold all the cake layers – when you lift the whisk, the cream should form peaks. Transfer to the fridge to chill.

Place a large, non-stick frying pan/skillet over a medium heat and lightly grease with vegetable oil. Add a ladleful of the cake mixture to the middle of the pan and tilt the pan so that the batter makes an even pancake. Place a lid on top and fry for 1½ minutes. Remove the lid, flip the cake and place the lid on top for another 1 minute. Carefully lift the cake from the pan and place on a wire rack to cool. Repeat with the remaining mixture to create four layers.

Fill a piping/pastry bag (or food bag with a small corner snipped off) with the chilled cream filling.

When the cake layers are completely cool, coat the first cake with an even layer of cream and top with strawberries. Repeat for each layer. Finish with any remaining cream and strawberries on top and use a sieve to lightly dust extra icing sugar all over. Enjoy immediately!

INDEX

GLOSSARY

Anju foods eaten with alcohol

Banchan side dishes

Bingsu shaved/grated frozen milk

Buchu garlic chives

Buchu jeon chive pancakes

Cheong syrups made from preserving fruits and vegetables in sugar

Chojang spicy dipping sauce made from gochujang and vinegar

Dashima dried kelp

Dangmyun sweet potato noodles

Danmuji Korean yellow pickled radish

Doenjang Korean soy bean paste

Doenjang jjigae soy bean paste stew

Eomuk/odeng Korean fish cakes

Garae tteok Korean cylindrical rice cakes

Gim seaweed sheets

Gochujang Korean red pepper paste

Gochugaru Korean red pepper flakes

Guk quick light soup

Hotteok sweet filled pancakes

Hwachae fruit punch

Hwe raw fish

Jang fermented soy products

Japchae stir-fried sweet potato noodles with vegetables

Jjigae Korean stew of meat, seafood or vegetables

Jjajjang black beans

Jjajjangmyeon black bean noodles

Jjambbong spicy noodle soup, usually seafood

Jeon savoury pancakes

Jumeokbap Korean rice balls

Juk rice porridge

Kalguksu knife-cut noodle soup

Kimbap seaweed rice roll

Makgeolli Korean rice wine

Mandu Korean dumplings

Mak kimchi cut cabbage kimchi

Milmyeon wheat noodles served in a cold broth

Mookeunji kimchi aged and fermented kimchi

Naengmyeon buckwheat noodles served in a cold broth

Ojingeo dried squid

Pajeon spring onion/scallion pancakes

Pajeori spring onion/scallion seasoned salad

Poggi kimchi whole cabbage kimchi

Ramyun Korean-style instant noodles

Samgyeopsal barbecued pork belly

Soju Korean spirit

Somyun thin wheat noodles

Soondae Korean blood sausage

Ssam refers to dishes that come wrapped in other foods, such as lettuce or other leafy vegetables

Sujebi hand-torn dumplings in broth

Tteokbokki rice cakes cooked in a spicy sauce

Yangnyeom jang soy seasoning sauce

ACKNOWLEDGEMENTS

It takes a whole team to create a book and I wouldn't have been able to do this without some amazing help. Thank you to Clare for taking such beautiful pictures – you have a real eye for detail and I loved working with you (and really hope we can go for lunch at that Korean place soon!) Jen, you have such an effortless skill with food styling, I feel like I learnt so much from watching you work your magic. Lola, thank you for working so hard – I hope you continue to use the recipes in this book to harness your love of kimchi and tteokbokki! Thank you to everyone at RPS for really believing in this book, but a special mention to Megan and Abi. Megan, you have been so patient with me and have created something so wonderful! Abi, thank you for that first email and for bringing this book to life.

My lovely agent Anna – I couldn't ask for better and I'm so thankful to be able to turn to you for your advice and expertise, even after all these years!

Rachel, thank you for being such a good friend and for helping me eat all the recipe-tests! You've been there through some challenging times and I'm thankful for our friendship and many coffee dates.

To our friends and family who have always helped us so much, but especially during my time in hospital. Thank you for your many messages, hospital visits, food deliveries – you kept us sane.

To the incredible NHS staff that helped me during my stint in hospital (and afterwards), thank you. You are inspirational and real life superheroes – I count myself lucky every day that I'm able to live my life normally now, thanks to you.

Mum and dad, thank you for being so supportive and being there when we need you. To Gareth, my best friend and chief taste tester – thank you for always taking care of us, believing in me and being my rock. To our wonderful boys – thank you for being my biggest champions and for always being so positive. I hope you can use this book to recreate a taste of home, even when you're all grown up.

And lastly, to everyone that has bought this book, thank you!